FREEDOM INSIGHTS

*demon*SPEAK

Recognising and overcoming the enemy voices in your life

GRAHAM WILSON

WSP
WILD SIDE PUBLISHING
real stories. real hope.

Published by Graham Wilson
Copyright © 2020 Graham C.R. Wilson
Email: liberationmanual@gmail.com

All rights reserved. This book is protected by the copyright laws of New Zealand. This book may not be copied or reprinted for commercial gain. The use of short quotations or occasional page copying for personal or group study is permitted.

Unless otherwise stated, Scripture references are taken from The Holy Bible, New International Version, copyright © 1973, 1978, 1984 by the International Bible Society. Scripture quotations marked The Passion Translation (TPT) are taken from The Passion Translation, © 2017 by Passion & Fire Ministries Inc.

Cover design: Wild Side Publishing
Text layout: Graham Wilson
Self-publishing assistance: Wild Side Publishing

Cataloguing in Publication Data:

Title: demonSPEAK

ISBN: 978-0-473-53462-2 (pbk)
      978-0-473-53463-9 (epub)

Subjects: Christian, Non-Fiction, New Zealand, Christian Living, Inspiration, Spirituality, Body Soul Spirit

First New Zealand printing, August 2020, www.benefitz.co.nz

International listing, Ingram Spark August 2020

www.wildsidepublishing.com

CONTENTS

Foreword v

Acknowledgements vii

Introduction 1

It's a War Out There 5

Uncovering the Lie 17

Condemnation 37

Anxiety 53

Discouragement 65

Mission 85

Temptation and Sin 99

Suffering 111

Light and Darkness 119

Marriage and Relationships 125

Unforgiveness 133

Conclusion 149

ENDORSEMENTS

If you have ever been assaulted by seemingly random negative thoughts then this is the book for you. It's filled with practical advice that can be immediately implemented. The book helps the reader to discern truth and lies — for example, when are the voices we are hearing the Holy Spirit bringing conviction, and when are they from the enemy? It's loaded with scripture and a powerful tool for anyone looking for freedom. This book is the perfect guide to see yourself set free and becoming all that God intended for you.

Anna Ho | www.reconciledworld.org
Executive Director | Reconciled World International

This is a really helpful book from a man who has walked the talk for decades as a counsellor, pastor, supervisor and soul friend to many. He has walked with the broken and marginalised, those called to cross-cultural mission, those involved in leadership and everyday 'normal' people just doing life. I wish I had this book twenty years ago — just for the chapter on discouragement. This is a training manual to find freedom — to take thoughts captive, to recognise the destructive source of so much of what is going on in our heads and to find a way out the other side. Graham is a gifted communicator so it is easy to read and make sense of, and his life and testimony proves it works. I will return to this book as a workbook. This is like a take-home life coach for doing well in life and mental health.

Steve Graham | www.equipperscollege.com
Principal | Equippers College

FOREWORD

This book has been over a decade in the writing. Not because of its length – in fact it is fairly brief. Not because of lack of material – it has all been there over that time. I have received encouragement from many people, including my long-suffering wife Lynda. I have had several prophetic "get that book done" words. I have heard from others how helpful the material has been to them. Yet I have struggled to bring it completion. My sister Karen, who is an experienced writer, recently went overseas and left me with the challenge to have a completed hard copy of the manuscript on her desk before she returned. I am happy to report that those words seemed to have been the veritable straw that broke the camel's back of this resistance to it being finished. She mentioned to me that books are never finished, just abandoned. That was of some help to me. And now I find myself writing this introduction having completed or abandoned the task. I got a text from my wife on hearing of my progress which read, "Awesome! Mega awesome!"

I write from a biblical Christian perspective. If that is not currently your worldview, you may find some of the language and concepts here a little unusual. Something has caused you to pick up this book through, so read on, check it out, you may be pleasantly surprised at what you find.

I offer this book not as a "do this and you will get that" life manual. Life and human beings are way too complex for that! I present it in the hope that some lights will go on for you and that you will receive insights which enable you on your journey into joy, freedom and a fruitful life with transformed ways of thinking. I also hope that you will have further glimpses into just how much you are loved by God and how completely Jesus' work on the cross has provided for your wellbeing and your impact on the wellbeing of others in your world.

If you catch some glimpses, gain some liberating insights that help you identify and overcome those enemy voices, if you come closer to Jesus, then the book will have accomplished its purpose.

My prayer is that in your reading you will encounter Jesus in a deeper and deeper way.

Yahoo! Have fun.

Graham Wilson

July 2020

ACKNOWLEDGEMENTS

My wife Lynda. After all these years it is finally done. For all your input and for the nearly 50 years of walking together on this faith journey.

My sister Karen and brother-in-law David, for all your help and for motivating me to finish.

My friend Roselle, for all the work you have done formatting, editing, encouraging and giving the push to this being completed.

The many people who have encouraged, prophesied, prayed and provoked me to get it done.

And of course, the Big Three — Father, Son and Holy Spirit.

Thank you!

INTRODUCTION

"Nothing terribly good ever happens to the Wilsons."

Wilson is my family name, and this was the "family motto" I grew up with.

My parents didn't intentionally give it to me, yet this is what became part of me from the life and times of growing up as Graham Wilson.

With the motto came associated ideas of poverty, mediocrity, being somehow "less than" and generally low self-esteem. It affected my confidence, caused me to achieve way less than I might have at school, saw me bullied by people smaller than myself, and had me leaving school at 15 years old rather than pursuing higher education.

Not a great foundation for a life of faith and hope!

Our sense of self affects all areas of our lives. However, I became a follower of Jesus when I was sixteen. His transforming work in my life began. It wasn't long before this family motto began to clash with His work in my life and my involvement in Jesus' purposes for my life.

My first ministry experience saw me involved in youth work, leading to employment in that role at a growing church. As the church grew and I got older, the youth ministry was handed over to younger people who took it onward and upward. I found myself moving into other roles, one of which was being in charge of the church's finances.

Now this idea of poverty and "nothing terribly good happens to the Wilsons" on the one hand and being in charge of church finances on the other hand was an interesting mix. There would inevitably be times during the year when finances were down, and things were looking grim. During those times I would have thoughts that went, "This is happening because YOU are in charge of it. If someone for whom good things did happen were in charge this wouldn't be happening." It was an undermining, self-hating thought pattern that I would have to battle against.

I also found myself feeling intimidated by people who seemed wealthy and successful, and because of this I was not as free as I might have been in speaking into their lives for their good, as God had intended me to do. This idea of being "less than" was a real hindrance.

I have coined a phrase to describe thoughts like these: "demonspeak".

Introduction

The pages ahead are intended to be an exposé of the strategies of demonspeak, and a resource to arm you in your journey of overcoming those strategies.

I am pleased to report that the "Nothing Terribly Good" motto has been pretty much obliterated from my life now. It may momentarily faintly whisper at particularly vulnerable times in my life, but it is easily silenced. It has been replaced with a healthy expectation of good things! Instead of being captured by that poverty spirit, God has used me to inspire and lead people into giving well in excess of a million dollars into missions over the past 20 years. His amazing grace has not only set me free, but He has also used me to be a part of other people coming into freedom in this area. Our Heavenly Father is awesome, and He often uses us to bring freedom to others in the very areas we have previously struggled with. All honour and praise to Him!

I will be referring to the Bible often in this book, mostly from the NIV version. The Bible is the ultimate Liberation Manual. Its truth will lead you into real freedom.

My hope and prayer is that from your experience with this book, as you recognise and overcome the undermining enemy thoughts in your own life, you will gain insights that bring you to a place of freedom, and that this will result in freedom flowing through you to others.

They will make captives of their captors
and rule over their oppressors.
Isaiah 14:2

We take captive every thought
to make it obedient to Christ.
2 Corinthians 10:5

IT'S A WAR OUT THERE

So then, prepare your hearts and minds for action! Stay alert and fix your hope firmly on the marvellous grace that is coming to you.

1 Peter 1:13a
(The Passion Translation)

The Battle

I wonder what caused you to pick up this book.

I wonder what undermining thoughts you have already identified in your life as you have begun to read.

Thoughts that bring you down.

Thoughts that sabotage your success.

Thoughts that hinder you from living freely and joyfully.

You may be a bit freaked out by the title of this book and talk about the devil and demons and their activity. From a biblical point of view, they are indeed real beings, intent on spoiling our lives. However, this is not as scary as it first appears.

When we speak of the enemy's efforts against our wellbeing, it is important to not inflate the devil and his forces in our minds. It is accurate to say that most of us will never hear from the devil himself. He is only ever in one place at one time and he is busy with some significantly greater threats to his wellbeing than you or me. Only God is everywhere at once. The Bible is clear that the devil and his demons are created finite beings. They are actually defective angels. Jesus totally overwhelmed and disempowered them at the cross.

The Bible does not present us with a "Star Wars" picture of reality where equally powerful dark and light sides of the force are in competition. The biblical reality is of Jesus, the uncreated creator; the first cause, Himself uncaused; the one who has defeated death and hell; the one whose name is above every other name. On the other side of the equation are some created beings.

The Bible is clear that our enemy the devil doesn't have any "dynamite" power to harm us. He does not have the power to overwhelm us and force us to do things. Jesus totally dealt with that at the cross. Look at what these verses from our *Liberation Manual* tell us:

> *Since the children have flesh and blood, He too shared in their humanity so that by His death He might destroy him who holds the power of death – that is, the devil – and free those who all their lives were held in slavery by their fear of death.*
> Hebrews 2:14-15
>
> *And having disarmed the powers and authorities, He made a public spectacle of them, triumphing over them by the cross.*
> Colossians 2:15

The enemy has no power to force you to do anything. Jesus totally disempowered him at the cross. He does, however, have the ability to influence or trick us. Paul, when writing to the Corinthians, ends his discussion about the issue of forgiveness and obedience with reference to satan's schemes. May you and I no longer be unaware of his little tricks. They are just that: schemes and tricks.

> ...*In order that satan might not outwit us.*
> *For we are not unaware of his schemes.*
> 2 Corinthians 2:11
>
> *Put on the full armour of God so that you can take your stand against the devil's schemes.*
> Ephesians 6:11

Again, here in this wonderful passage about spiritual warfare, the reference is not to some incredible power the enemy has, but to his schemes, his tricks. He is empowered in our lives when we believe his lies, and by our lack of awareness of his strategies.

The Battlefield

This negative, ungodly influence comes mainly in the area of our thinking. In fact, the huge majority of personal spiritual warfare happens in our minds.

Negative enemy thoughts are planted in our minds and over time, if entertained, become entrenched "strongholds" in our lives, sometimes built on hereditary, "handed down" ways of being and thinking. These thoughts are often built on painful life experiences and the meaning we have been tricked into investing in them.

During the limited amount of work I have done with childhood abuse survivors, one of the keys to them moving forward has been helping them to reinterpret the evil destructive words and actions they have suffered at the hand of adults. The idea that they were, indeed, somehow responsible or deserving of the abuse often lodges itself within. It is powerful to see these people consciously affirm that the abuse was not about them, nor in any way their fault, and that they are in no way responsible for any evil inflicted on them.

The enemy works hard on having us make and continue to hold inaccurate interpretations of what has happened to us. But God equips us to identify, expose and demolish these strongholds in our minds and hearts!

Let's look again to our *Liberation Manual*.

> *For though we live in the world, we do not wage war as the world does. The weapons we fight with are not the weapons of the world.*
>
> *On the contrary, they have divine power to demolish strongholds We demolish arguments and every pretension that sets itself up against the knowledge of God, and we take captive every thought to make it obedient to Christ.*
> 2 Corinthians 10:3-5

The term "pretension" is used here. One definition of pretension is "creating a false appearance of great importance or worth". It is a foundation-less idea, a false thought, a deception or lie. These demonspeak thoughts that we contend with are, in the light of the truth of scripture, foundation-less false thoughts, fairy tales, or lies. Our task is to identify them, take them captive and make them obey Jesus Christ who is The Truth.

This is where we fight and win the battle, by taking every thought captive and making it obey Christ. This scripture has become a "life scripture" to me – a new "family motto"! Instead of struggling with enemy thoughts I now, by the grace of God, find myself empowering others to overcome in this area.

Our future can be one of transformed, renewed thinking, as these following verses tell us.

> *Be made new in the attitude of your minds...*
> Ephesians 4:23

> *Do not conform any longer to the pattern of this world but be transformed by the renewing of your mind. Then you will be able to test and approve what God's will is – His good, pleasing and perfect will.*
> Romans 12:2

As we win the battle of the mind, we find incredible personal freedom and are released to impact others in a whole new way. I wonder whose freedom waits on the other side of your transformation.

The Move

When I am speaking with people about this, I teach them the demonspeak martial arts type move! Maybe you would like to try it. Do it slowly at first, so as not to hurt yourself...

> Stretch out your right hand to the side.
>
> Bring it up to your temple.
>
> Close your hand in a grabbing motion (taking the thought captive).

Bring your hand down quickly, opening your hand (throwing the thought on the ground).

Stamp on it with your right foot saying, "Obey in Jesus' name!"

Try to avoid doing this in public, as it may concern people around you!

This is, of course, a fun physical activity done to reinforce in our minds that we are to take thoughts captive.

Many of the thoughts and entrenched beliefs that bring and keep us down have been there for long enough for them to go unnoticed. They are just part of our background head traffic. They feel quite normal. There is often a whirlwind of thoughts buzzing around in our head, or an old persistent refrain of defectiveness or unworthiness playing there. Our head can be a very busy place! Noticing and identifying these thought patterns and taking them captive is crucial to our freedom.

As I interact with people about their thoughts, I am fascinated to see that when they describe their troubling, accusing, downing thoughts, they often motion towards their heads with their hands. As we interact further, they begin to talk about what they really know, and their hand will often go to their chest area. Deeper than the tumult of thoughts in your head is the truth of God in your heart. As we begin to take the thoughts captive, the storm subsides, and we are more able to link into what we know from Jesus. An old dear friend and mentor of mine would often say, "Sack the committee in your head!"

A powerful practical way to take thoughts captive is to write them down. This traps them in one space, rather than having them swirling around in your head. Having written them down, then write the truth next to them. Write some verses from the *Liberation Manual* (the Bible) that contradict these thoughts. It can also be helpful to make a list of "witnesses": people who would agree with these thoughts about yourself, and those who would disagree. You might like to start the disagree list with Father, Son and Holy Spirit, and then others in your life who love you and want your best. We will most often find that the list of accusers is quite short compared to that list headed up by the Big Three.

At key strategic times in my life, some demonic thoughts will often come wafting in. Maybe I am about to preach a word that I feel God has put on my mind for that time. I will be joining in worship and praise to God with everyone else, and then a thought comes seemingly out of nowhere. It may be some unwelcome images from the past, or some painful past experience, or some unanswered prayer (with the associated feeling) aiming to pull me down and undermine me. It may come up as you are about to embark on a project, try something new, or head off into a new social setting; suddenly you are assailed by undermining thoughts whittling away at your sense of self, of confidence, and the sense of joy you might otherwise expect to have at such times.

My friend recently told me of waking up in the early hours of a Sunday morning when I had left him responsible for running the church service while I was away. He said he woke with a real emotional heaviness and with thoughts like these: "You're not worthy to be leading today. You have no right to be there. God is not going to use you today. You have nothing to say, nothing to offer. Who do you think you are?"

I wonder if you recognise any of this from your own life.

My friend was experienced enough to recognise where these thoughts and feelings came from, to see that they were just an attack of the enemy, and to deal quickly with them.

It has been said that it is pretty difficult to stop birds landing on your head, but it is foolish to let them start nesting there. You can tell where bids are nesting because there are a lot of bird droppings everywhere. These thoughts are like birds unexpectedly landing on your head. Don't give them a chance to get comfortable!

The good news is that you are not sentenced to receiving all the crappy thinking that comes and attacks your mind. That is not God's will for you. God wants to release you and empower you to take those thoughts captive and make them obey. It's true! God says in His Word that we can be transformed by the renewing of our minds. You can have incredible control over your thoughts! As we get hold of this and start to put it into action, it will be transformational.

> *Reflection:* What has stood out to you from this section?
> What is happening for you as you think about these things?

Imagine a life where you are able to "take every thought captive and make it obey Christ".

This book is intended to do two things: to expose the way the enemy seeks to undermine us and bring us down via our thoughts, and to resource you with understandings and strategies that empower you to overcome his destructive work.

The reason the Son of God appeared was to destroy and undo what the devil has done.
1 John 3:8b

UNCOVERING THE LIE

When he (the devil) lies,
he speaks his native language,
for he is a liar and the father of lies.

John 8:44b

Recognising the Counterfeit

People often ask me how you can tell if a thought is good or bad. Asking that question is an excellent start on your pathway into freedom. One of my prayers is that this book will sensitise you to the thoughts coming at you. It is so important that we examine and question the thoughts that come to us. Do they seem healthy or unhealthy? Godly or ungodly? Scriptural or unscriptural? From where are they sourced? Do they sound like the voice of the Holy Spirit or some demon spirit?

I have heard that federal agents learn to spot counterfeit banknotes by spending a lot of time looking not at counterfeit notes, but rather at the real article. They become so aware of what the genuine looks and feels like that they instantly recognise the counterfeit. As we immerse ourselves in the truth of God's Word ("GodSpeak") it prepares us to recognise demonspeak when it comes.

Most currency has a transparent watermark on it that becomes more visible as it is held up to the light. Let's look now at some of the basic truths of our *Liberation Manual* – the watermarks of "GodSpeak" – to help us recognise whether the thoughts that come to us are informed by heaven or by hell.

The Work of the Holy Spirit

But when He, the Spirit of truth, comes, He will guide you into all truth. He will not speak on His own; He will speak only what He hears, and He will tell you what is yet to come. He will bring glory to me by taking from what is mine and making it known to you.

John 16:13-14

For you did not receive a spirit that makes you a slave again to fear, but you received the Spirit of sonship. And by Him we cry, "Abba, Father." The Spirit Himself testifies with our spirit that we are God's children.

Romans 8:15-16

Understanding the work and nature of the Holy Spirit is foundational to us recognising the origin of the thoughts that come to us. The Holy Spirit was given to us when Jesus left this earth and went to heaven. He lives inside every follower of Jesus. What the Holy Spirit says and does absolutely aligns with what Jesus and the Father say and do. They are One!

This is what the Bible tells us the Holy Spirit's activities are:

- ✓ convicting people about sin, righteousness and judgement
- ✓ comforting and helping us
- ✓ leading us into all truth
- ✓ revealing more to us about Jesus
- ✓ telling us that we belong to the family of God
- ✓ revealing to us everything God has for us
- ✓ gifting us to bless others
- ✓ causing certain fruit (ways of being) to grow in our lives
- ✓ leading us and guiding us
- ✓ empowering us as witnesses of Jesus.

When the Holy Spirit speaks to us, what He says and how He says it will be consistent with who He is and what He is given to us for. This is a powerful filter through which to put the thoughts that come to you.

> **Question:** Does this thought feel and sound like it is from the One who is there to help and comfort me; the One who encourages me that I am a child of God; the One who reveals all the amazing things God has for me?

Life

The Spirit gives life, the flesh counts for nothing; the words I have spoken to you are spirit and they are life.
John 6:63

I have come to give you life, in all its fullness.
John 10:10

One of the fundamental understandings that we have about God speaking to us is that His words are spirit and they are life. Have you ever been convicted by God about something? Even in the midst of deep conviction, when God speaks to us it is full of life and it is full of motivation to change. It energises us! The "fear of the Lord", that awestruck sense of wonder, makes us turn from sin.

When the enemy speaks to us, it is like a wet blanket. Have you ever been under condemnation, instead of under conviction? You may have had thoughts like some of these:

- "What a hopeless Christian you are."
- "You'd better not go to a small group – if you ever get involved in a group, they will find out what you're really like and you'll be put out of the church!"
- "You wouldn't be having communion if they knew what sort of Christian you were."
- "What do you mean witness to your friends? Look at you!"

Words like these have no life and no motivation. They just bring a generalised, downward paralysis. When you are hearing from God, it motivates you. It builds life; it doesn't bring death. His words are spirit and life.

> **Questions:** Are these thoughts energising and motivating me to change?
> Are they bringing life to me, or death?

Freedom

> *You will know the truth and the truth will set you free.*
> John 8:32
>
> *It is for freedom that Christ has set us free.*
> Galatians 5:1
>
> *If the Son sets you free, you will be free indeed.*
> John 8:36

When Jesus speaks to us, it brings freedom; it releases us to live life more fully. The enemy, on the other hand, loves to try to dupe us with religious thoughts that separate us from other people and trap us into legalistic or weird ways of living, or with thoughts that lead us into destructive, sinful ways of living. Both of these paths lead to entrapment.

I remember as a young, passionate Christian doing a short stint in a Bible college. One visiting speaker was a powerful, deep-voiced communicator. He said that if we were not reading twenty chapters of the Bible a day, we were probably not real Christians. Unbelievably this really hit me, and I found myself doubting my salvation. What this speaker said sounded virtuous:

demonSPEAK

God does want us to be reading His Word. It is, after all, our *Liberation Manual*. The speaker's statement, though, was religious and certainly not from heaven! A death-bringing religious demon started attacking me through those words. Fortunately, this only lasted a few days until God's amazing grace and love regained their rightful place in my life.

I once heard someone say that many of us live in constricting fear of somehow missing the will of God for our lives. It is as if we must walk a very fine line of His will, like walking a tightrope. What if I make a wrong decision? What if I marry the wrong person? He suggested that the will and purposes of God are more like a playground than a tightrope. God is there walking with us in the options we take, taking any mistakes we may make and working them for good. That was a very helpful picture for me. Jesus intends our life in Him to be full of adventure and joy, not fear that we may put a foot wrong.

> ***Question:*** Where are these thoughts taking me?
>   Into life and freedom?

Righteousness

He leads me in paths of righteousness for His name's sake.

Psalm 23:3

God cannot be tempted by evil, nor does He tempt anyone.

James 1:13

Disastrous, sinful life choices begin with a thought that is entertained in our minds. James (1:14) calls this being enticed and dragged away by evil desire. Marital infidelity, for instance, is the result of an accumulation of "entertained" thoughts that have resulted in action.

The initial thought of attraction or "it would be wonderful to be with her (or him)", if not taken captive, will take root in your life and end in action. The tempting "I wonder what it would be like to..." questions can lead to disaster. Here, the old saying that curiosity killed the cat rings true.

My old friend and mentor used to encourage people to ask the question, "And then what?" This is an excellent question to ask of a thought that comes to us. What would happen after I did that? Where will this path lead me?

I once attended a seminar that was dealing with the topic of sexual addiction. The speaker told of a man who had a recurring fantasy about having an affair with the woman who lived next door. The two families were close friends and he was feeling attracted to her.

The therapist had him describe the fantasy playing out, asking "and then what?" at each step. Once past the actual adulterous act, the questions led to the outcomes: going back home to his wife and family with this secret; the awkwardness of future interactions with their close friends; the whole affair finally coming out; the hurt that would cause to his wife, the children involved, and the friendship. It was a sobering discussion. The excitement of the moment was contrasted with the extreme cost.

> ***Questions:*** Are there thoughts nudging me onto a path of righteousness?
> And then what?

Led, not Driven

> *The shepherd calls his own sheep by name and leads them out. He goes on ahead of them and his sheep follow him, because they know his voice.*
> John 10:3-4

Jesus refers to Himself as the Good Shepherd. He goes before us and leads us. This is an important point. The picture here is of the eastern shepherd who calls his sheep by name. This contrasts with the New Zealand shepherd, who whistles up his dog to bark and nip at the sheep until they get into line. Most religious delusion has a large component of drivenness in it. People have done outrageous, unthinkable things because "God told them to". Our psychiatric wards are full of such people. There are terrible stories of harassment, drivenness and torment. That is never how God speaks. We have some very fine, religious-sounding thoughts that are really like dogs barking and "biting our backside", driving us.

When Jesus leads you, He goes before you and says, "Come on, let's do this. Come on, come with me!" There's a togetherness, not a driving that says, "Get out there!"

Some of us have grown up with "please don't send me to Africa" thoughts, that the very place you don't want to go is the place where God will send you, or that God will make you marry someone you find repulsive. It's a similar sort of thing, this idea of a God who drives you to do what you do not want to do. This is absolutely not our Heavenly Father's character at all!

> **Questions:** Are these thoughts harassing and driving me, or is there a "personal invitation" encouraging me to come and follow?

Jesus' Sacrifice is Absolutely Enough! You are Going to Make It!

"My name is Wilsy and God is up off His throne, singing and dancing over me!"

One of my nicknames used to be Wilsy. One day, after I had preached from Zephaniah, I arrived at work to find that my friend Merylene, a church music director, had put that sign on my office door. This is a much healthier life motto!

Here is my paraphrase of Zephaniah 3:14-17:

> *Sing and shout aloud, sons and daughters of God!*
> *Be glad and rejoice with all your heart.*
> *The Lord has taken away your punishment,*
> *He has turned back your enemy.*
> *The Lord is with you; never again will you fear any harm.*
> *Do not fear, you people of God*
> *The Lord is with you! He is mighty to save!*

He will take great delight in you!
He will quiet you with His love,
He will rejoice over you with singing!

Here, at the end of the Old Testament, is the gospel summed up in a few verses.

Because of what Jesus has done we are free to sing, shout and rejoice. The punishment we were due has been taken away. The enemy has been defeated and turned back. Our all-powerful Jesus is with us, so we do not need to be afraid. The Lord delights in us, He quiets and comforts us in His love, He rejoices over us with singing.

This is a foundational "watermark" of God speaking to us.

As we take hold of this fact, that what Jesus accomplished in His death, burial and resurrection is absolutely more than enough to reconcile us to God and cover all of our sins and shortcomings, that truth becomes a great filter to sift out demonspeak thoughts that come to us. Your sins are totally forgiven!

> *God has made you alive with Christ. He has forgiven us **all** our sins, taking away the list of charges against us, nailing it to the cross.*
> Colossians 2: 13-14

> *Because Jesus lives forever, He is able to save completely those who come to God through Him, because He always lives to intercede for them.*
> Hebrews 7:24-25
>
> *By one sacrifice Jesus has made perfect forever those who are being made holy.*
> Hebrews 10:14
>
> *When He had received the drink, Jesus said, "It is finished." With that, He bowed His head and gave up His spirit.*
> John 19:30

Jesus is able to save you completely. He is on your side, praying for you in heaven. In fact, in God's mind you are already perfect, the finished product. He is enjoying the process of you "becoming".

Another picture the Bible paints of how God sees us is this: that in Christ, we have died to sin and are now raised to new life in Him. Baptism is described in those terms in Romans chapter 6. Now, that is a "job complete" picture of us!

Ephesians chapter 2 pictures us seated with Christ in the heavenly realms, at the right hand of the Father, far above all rule, power and authority, over all titles that can be given, with everything under His feet!

Before you ask, I have no idea how all this works. The truth of these scriptures is not so much to be understood with our minds as embraced with our whole being. Learn to say "yes and amen" to the word of God without necessarily fully understanding how it can be.

"How does that all work?" is a good prayer to pray. The Holy Spirit has been given to us in order to reveal to us all that God has for us. I love these words from an old hymn:

> Make me understand it,
> Help me to take it in,
> What it meant for you,
> The Holy One,
> To take away my sin.

Now may the God of peace Himself sanctify you completely; and may your whole spirit, soul, and body be preserved blameless at the coming of our Lord Jesus Christ. He who calls you is faithful, who also will do it.
1 Thessalonians 5:23-24

> **Questions:** Are these thoughts encouraging me that I am forgiven, that Jesus is with me, that I am going to make it?
> Are these thoughts filling me with confidence and joy that Jesus is with me?
> Are these thoughts bringing me into a deeper appreciation of God's love?

Toning Up

I am a passable basic guitar and ukulele player. However, there was a drawback in my early attempts to learn the guitar, which brought some pain and amusement to my brother-in-law who was helping me to learn: I was totally tone deaf. I could not tell if my guitar was in or out of tune and could blissfully play in one key while singing in another. I just could not tell!

Our thoughts have tone too, but until we pay attention, we are unaware of their tone. As I listen to people describe their thoughts to me, they naturally apply tone to them. They may be sarcastic, accusative, grizzly, critical, self-hateful, fearful, angry, malicious, insulting, mocking. As we begin on this path of taking every thought captive, listening for the "tone" of our thoughts will be a real give-away of demonspeak.

Jesus' voice is not grizzly, accusative, sarcastic, malicious or hateful. Jesus does not mock us, put us down, or accuse us. You will not hear Jesus say, "loser", "idiot", or "no-hoper".

> *Jesus' sheep follow Him because they know His voice. But they will never follow a stranger; in fact, they will run away from him, because they do not recognise a stranger's voice.*
> John 10:4-5

It is God's intention for us that we become so attuned to His voice that we easily recognise when it is **not** Him speaking to us.

Questions: Do these thoughts sound like they come from Jesus who totally paid the price for my forgiveness and transformation?
Do these thoughts sound like they come from God who delights in me, and already sees me as complete in Christ?
Who are you going to believe?

> *Jesus became flesh and dwelt among us. He was full of grace and truth.*
> John 1:14

demonSPEAK

> *The devil was a murderer from the beginning, not holding to the truth, for there is no truth in him. When he lies, he speaks his native language, for he is a liar and the father of lies.*
> John 8:44

The choice is ours. Who will we believe? Which thoughts will we give "airtime" to in our heads?

Jesus is full of truth — He is "**The** Truth". The devil is full of lies.

As we commit to taking every thought captive, and we become more aware of the negative demonspeak thoughts that come our way, we can encourage ourselves with the knowledge that there is no truth in the devil, that he only speaks lies. It follows, then, that the demonspeak thoughts that assail us are actually lies, untruths, and foundation-less accusations.

Application: One powerful way of taking thoughts captive is to write them down. Writing them traps them on the page and allows you to examine them. Try beginning a journal, recording some of the demonspeak thoughts you find. Begin to write scriptures (GodSpeak) next to them. Make them obey!

A Prayer

Lord, I bring my mind to you. Transform me by renewing my mind.

I choose to believe your descriptions of who I am and what I can do.

Increase my awareness of the thoughts that come to me.

Help me to take captive every form of demon*speak and make it obey you.*

I give my heart mind and imagination to you afresh.

In Jesus' name!

Let's look now at some more specific areas of battle with demonspeak.

CONDEMNATION

There is now no condemnation
to those in Christ Jesus.

Romans 8:1

I remember some years ago visiting a small village in Aceh, the northernmost province of Indonesia. Down the middle of the main street came a woman bleeding from a head wound. On each side of the street were people shouting abuse at her. It was a terrible situation. I can only imagine how she must have felt.

Accused.

Exposed.

Miserable.

Isolated.

Unloved.

Shamed.

Excluded.

It reminded me of a story from the earthly ministry of Jesus in John 8:2-11.

A woman caught in adultery is brought before Jesus. She was probably in some state of undress and was dragged into the temple courts while Jesus was teaching and made to stand before the group. Imagine being caught in some sinful situation, being dragged into church in the middle of the sermon and being stood up in front of the group.

Condemnation

She was exposed to public shame. As is often the case with religion, there is no mention of the man involved. Where was he? The crowd is not interested in justice or righteousness, not interested in her plight or her wellbeing. (We are certainly at our worst when we are being religious, especially when it is about someone else's sin!) This woman was simply being used as bait to trap Jesus.

What a picture of condemnation!

What a picture of where demonspeak would like us to be!

Jesus confronts the woman's accusers and dismisses them. He then forgives her and sends her on her way into a new way of living.

There is another story in similar vein in Zechariah 3:1-5.

Have you ever had one of those nasty dreams where you have turned up at school or some other public place and you suddenly realise that you have somehow forgotten to put on some or all of your clothes, and there you are exposed to the world! Here in the book of Zechariah is a story of Joshua the high priest in the presence of God, dressed really inappropriately. Satan is there, accusing him. The devil is actually known as the "accuser of the brethren". The Lord rebukes satan, affirms Joshua, dresses him in new "rich garments", and commissions him to ministry and a place of standing among his peers.

Contrast these exposés of condemnation with Jesus' attitudes and actions to the woman, and to Joshua. The enemy uses condemnation to isolate us, shame us and destroy our sense of self. Jesus, on the other hand, comes into our times of failure with forgiveness, cleansing, and words that build our sense of identity in Him, that instruct us and release us into a life of freedom and fruitfulness.

Contrast these stories of condemnation with the account of Isaiah's conviction encounter with the Lord in Isaiah 6:1-9.

Isaiah sees the Lord in all His splendour and is immediately conscious of specific sin. There is no record of accusation or condemnation here, just an encounter with God's glory. Isaiah prays, confessing his sin and shortcomings. God answers him and provides a remedy, a specific encounter to deal with the issue that Isaiah confesses, and then commissions him to get on with the call God has put on his life.

Compare these stories with the words of Jesus to the churches in Revelation (chapters 2-3). When He brings correction to them, He is very specific about what needs to change, and He gives clear direction on what He wants them to do about it.

These stories highlight the differences between condemnation and the conviction of The Holy Spirit.

Condemnation is designed to destroy us.

Condemnation is generalised and totalising. It gives a feeling of being completely unclean and useless, full of shame.

Condemnation is accusing, tormenting, and paralysing. We are left feeling like just giving up.

Condemnation drives us downwards and seeks to shame us and drive us away from God.

Condemnation seeks to convince us that we are unworthy of His love and unfit for His service.

On the other hand:

Conviction is designed to transform us and set us free.

Conviction is specific, offers a remedy, and motivates us to action and change.

Conviction draws us to God and releases us to more freely be ourselves and give ourselves to Him and His purposes.

> *Godly sorrow brings repentance that leads to salvation and leaves no regret, but worldly sorrow brings death.*
> 2 Corinthians 7:9

Have a look at Isaiah 61:3-10. Here God's heart and intentions towards us are described. This is what God has for us in our low times, our times of failure:

- ✓ A crown of beauty instead of ashes.
- ✓ The oil of gladness instead of mourning.
- ✓ A garment of praise instead of a spirit of despair.
- ✓ A new sense of identity and purpose.
- ✓ A "double portion" instead of shame.
- ✓ A joyful inheritance instead of disgrace.
- ✓ Garments of salvation to clothe us.
- ✓ A robe of righteousness.

Read and reread these parts of scripture. Fill your mind with them! Our God doesn't condemn, but only desires to forgive, cleanse and set us free. How awesome is that!

Now look at Hebrews 4:14-16.

> *Therefore, since we have a great high priest who has gone through the heavens, Jesus the Son of God, let us hold firmly to the faith we profess. For we do not have a high priest who is unable to sympathise with our weaknesses, but we have one who has been tempted in every way, just as we are — yet was without sin. Let us then approach the throne of grace with confidence, so that we may receive mercy and find grace to help us in our time of need.*

Here we are invited, because of Jesus, to come before God filled with confidence, to receive mercy and grace in our time of need. What an invitation written to our times of failure!

I love the account of Peter's restoration in John 21:15-17. Peter has denied Jesus three times. He did it standing round a fire. Now Jesus sets up a similar scene where they are around a fire, and He gives Peter three opportunities to confess his love for Him. At each confession of his love, Jesus commissions Peter. Three denials replaced by three statements of love, and three commissionings to leadership. Amazing grace!

The following passage from Revelation tells us that the devil is the accuser of the people of God.

> *Now have come the salvation and the power*
> *and the kingdom of our God,*
> *and the authority of His Christ.*
> *For the accuser of our brothers,*
> *who accuses them before our God*
> *day and night,*
> *has been hurled down.*
> *They overcame him by the blood of the Lamb*
> *and by the word of their testimony;*
> *they were willing to lay down their lives for Jesus.*
> Revelation 12:10-12

I have a friend who is a follower of Jesus. He used to work as a storeman, and one of the departments he had to often go to had pictures of naked women plastering the walls. He would find these quite distracting. I remember him telling me one day that he had gone into the department, done what he needed to do, and had left without even glancing at those pictures. I was pretty excited for him! He then said that he had had the thought, "If you were any sort of Christian, you would have torn those pictures down from the wall!" He was actually feeling a bit disappointed in himself. As he told me the thoughts that came to him, the tone of his voice was accusative, critical, almost sneering. Instead of hearing the affirmation from his heavenly Father over a new victory won, he was ambushed by the voice of a religious demon. I was able to strongly encourage him that those were enemy thoughts, not sourced from heaven!

Do you get the picture? Those thoughts had a ring of "holiness" to them, but they were actually lies of the enemy, attacking my friend's sense of self and wellbeing, preventing him from celebrating a victory won. The voices of condemnation can often sound very "righteous and holy" to the untrained ear, yet in actual fact they are diametrically opposed to the real voice of God. They are not the sound of heaven.

When accusing thoughts come, you can be sure where they come from!

Some of us live with a constant, often background, chorus of condemning thoughts: "One day you will be exposed"; "someday people will see how incompetent you are" and the like.

We are told in the above scriptures from Revelation 12 that we overcome the enemy and his attempts at condemnation by the blood of the Lamb and the word of our testimony, and by continually surrendering our lives to Jesus. Let's take a closer look at these.

The Blood of the Lamb

Jesus' work on the cross is designed to free us from sin. Our life in Christ is one of being changed from one degree of glory to another to be like Him. While we are learning to take hold of every good thing He has for us, He has made provision for our failures — His blood poured out for us, and His ongoing intercession at the right hand of God for us.

> *If we walk in the light... the blood of Jesus purifies us from all sin. If we confess our sins, God is faithful and just. He will forgive our sins and make us clean from all unrighteousness.*
> 1 John 1:7,9

> *My dear children, I write this to you so that you will not sin. But if anybody does sin, we have one who speaks to the Father in our defence — Jesus Christ, the Righteous One. He is the atoning sacrifice for our sins, and not only for ours but also for the sins of the whole world.*
> 1 John 2:1-2

If some area of failure comes up in your life, confess it to Him and immediately receive His ongoing forgiveness and cleansing. Note that I said "receive" – we don't have to beg, make deals or promises, or anything like that. In my early years of walking with Jesus I was schooled in the idea that, if we truly repent and vow never to commit that sin again, then God will forgive us. But the Bible tells us that if we *confess* our sin, He will forgive us our sin, and even more than that, He will cleanse us from all unrighteousness. Every time we come to Him in confession, He forgives that sin, and a fresh flow of His blood cleanses every part of our being. Another level of freedom and transformation occurs. Just receive it from His open hands and heart! Jesus is there in "heaven central" as the sacrifice that paid for our sin, speaking on our behalf. As we truly embrace this free provision of His grace, our hearts will be softened towards His will and ways. We will grow more in love with Him and less in love with sin. This free forgiveness is offered so that we will not sin. Listen to the words of Psalm 130:3-4:

> *If You, O Lord, kept a record of sins,*
> *O Lord, who could stand?*
> *But with You there is forgiveness;*
> *therefore, You are to be feared.*

Our experience of His free forgiveness develops in us a growing sense of wonder towards Him — the fear of the Lord.

I have often been asked how many times we can go back to Jesus over the same area of failure and be forgiven.

My answer is: as many times as it takes for you to fall out of love with that thing and discover Jesus' way of overcoming in that area. As many times as it takes!

The Word of our Testimony

Become more and more active in sharing your faith with others. As we do this, we gain a greater and greater grasp on all that we have in Him.

> *I pray that you may be active in sharing your faith, so that you will have a full understanding of every good thing we have in Christ.*
> Philemon 1:6

Also align your spoken words with what the Bible says about you. Confessing aloud the promises of God is a key to overcoming the enemy.

"Thank you, Lord Jesus, that I belong to you."

"Thank you that you are completing the work you have begun in my life."

"Thank you that you are with me."

Continually Surrender your Life to Jesus

*I urge you because of God's great mercy,
to offer your bodies as living sacrifices.*
Romans 12:1

This is no doubt a reference to actual Christian martyrdom that many of our brothers and sisters face on a daily basis around the world. For those of us not faced with martyrdom, though, there is still an application of these verses: continually lay down your life before Him.

In Revelation 12:12 we are told that the devil is full of fury because he knows his time is short. As you and I grow in God, we will often find that every step further into the freedom God has for us will be accompanied by a flurry of opposition. Don't be surprised, and just see it as the enemy of your soul in a panicked frenzy because he knows his days are numbered.

The enemy accuses.

Jesus convicts, forgives, cleanses and sets us free into His purposes!

You may have noticed that the word shame has come up a few times. Shame is a known close associate of condemnation. It works away at convincing us that we are somehow defective, somehow "less than", that some time we will be discovered and exposed for the impostors that we really are. It brings a nagging thought and feeling that we don't and won't measure up, eroding our sense of self.

The truth is, we are all equally wonderful creations of our Father God. In Ephesians 2:10 we are described as God's workmanship, His crafted works created to be used by Him to bless this world. That is true also of you! We are all also flawed in so many ways by the effects of sin and brokenness. The *Liberation Manual* describes us as jars of clay containing valuable treasure. Someone has coined the phrase "wounded healers". Check out the songs "Beautifully Broken" by Plumb, and "Masterpiece" by David Dunn. God uses us in our brokenness, while transforming us from one degree to another into Jesus' image.

I recommend that for further insight and ammunition you read *The Soul of Shame* by Curt Thompson.

> ***Questions:*** Are these thoughts drawing me closer to Jesus?
> Do these thoughts sound like Jesus speaking to me?
> Are these thoughts motivating me to change?
> Are these thoughts releasing me further into the purposes of God?
> Do these thoughts make me want to go and proclaim how good God is?

ANXIETY

I am an old man,
and have known a great many troubles,
but most of them never happened.

Mark Twain

demonSPEAK

On the album *Monty Python Sings* there is a track entitled "I'm So Worried". It is an amusing song detailing all of the issues the person is worried about: current fashions, the environment, the shows they repeat on TV, down to whether the hearers will like the song. The chorus line is: "And I'm so worried about the baggage retrieval system they've got at Heathrow"! It is a real anxiety anthem!

Anxiety and worry are bad for our health, rob us of sleep, burn up emotional energy and interfere with our enjoyment of today.

> *Worry is interest paid on trouble before it is due!*
> My Grandma

> *Worry never robs tomorrow of its sorrow,*
> *it only saps today of its joy.*
> Leo Buscagli

> *Today is the tomorrow we worried about yesterday.*
> Anon

Let's take a look at what the Bible (GodSpeak) says about anxiety, and then move to the demonspeak of anxiety and how to defeat it.

At the end of Matthew chapter 6 we are told to not worry about tomorrow, for tomorrow will worry about itself; each day will have enough challenges of its own. These words of Jesus end a lengthy teaching on anxiety and worry. Let's extract the main points from the previous sixteen verses:

- ✓ Don't store up treasure on earth.
- ✓ Where your treasure is, there your heart will be also.
- ✓ Don't worry about life, food, drink, body, clothes.
- ✓ Your heavenly Father looks after the birds – you are more valuable than them.
- ✓ Does worrying add a single hour to your life?
- ✓ Don't worry!
- ✓ Your Heavenly Father knows what you need.
- ✓ Seek first His kingdom; He will look after you.
- ✓ Don't worry about tomorrow, today has enough trouble!

What do you think Jesus is trying get across to us here?!

The apostle Paul writes in a similar vein to the believers in Philippi.

> *Rejoice in the Lord always. Again, I say, rejoice! Don't be anxious about anything. In everything, with prayer and thanksgiving, present your requests to God. Then peace beyond understanding will guard you hearts and minds in Christ Jesus.*
> Philippians 4:4,6-7

Peter takes up the same theme in his letter to "God's scattered exiles":

> *Cast all your anxiety on Him, because He cares for you.*
> 1 Peter 5:7

And the prophet Isaiah brings a similar message:

> *You will keep in perfect peace him whose mind is steadfast, because he trusts in you.*
> Isaiah 26:3

Psalm 46 begins with the words that God is our refuge and strength, a constantly present help in times of trouble. The psalm then goes on to describe a world falling apart and God's actions in it. It then finishes with the instruction to be still and know that He is God, that He will be exalted in the earth. The wider meaning of "be still" is to let go, relax, cease striving. Picture that: in the midst of trouble, you are being still, letting go, relaxing, stopping striving. The last verse of this psalm tells us that the Lord Almighty is with us and that God is our fortress.

I remember a meeting we were hosting with a number of guests from outside of our church. A drunk man had turned up and was shadow boxing two ladies. I finally had to tell him to leave. He basically told me to come outside with him and he would sort me out. I remember following him out thinking that this was going to end up getting physical, and not being real comfortable with that. As we got to the door, this man went down the stairs of the church and then turned around to confront me. When he turned around, a look of real fear came over him and he quickly scurried off down the road. As well as being relieved, I also felt quite manly that he had been so afraid of me! In reality, two really big guys from my youth group had seen what was happening and had followed us out. When the drunk man turned around, he saw not only me, but these two scary looking guys standing behind me. While feeling a little deflated, I was really glad to have them there! I felt safe when they were with me.

How much more should we feel safe and free from anxiety and fear when the Lord Almighty is with us!

In Zephaniah 3:17 we are told that the Lord is with us like a mighty warrior. Imagine if, when you looked in the mirror in the morning, you saw Jesus standing behind you. You would tend to worry a whole lot less! He is with us!

The Bible's message about worry? DON'T!

Another song I really enjoy is Bobby McFerrin's "Don't Worry, Be Happy". There's a message there for those of us susceptible to anxiety.

I was recently talking to someone about anxiety, and I found myself saying that many of the things we worry about, we will look back on in the future and laugh about our anxiety. So why not laugh now? That would be a great T-shirt to get printed: LAUGH NOW!

Are you getting this? The message is don't worry. Instead, when faced with potentially worrisome events, we are to:

Rejoice

The apostle Paul says that rejoicing is a safeguard for us. My understanding of "rejoice" is simply to express praise and thanksgiving to God (whether or not you feel it at that moment) for His goodness, grace, love and power. Rejoice for the fact that He promises to be with you, that He goes before you, that He lives in you, that He is over you, that He is your rear guard — He has your back! Praise Him for His amazing grace that is more than sufficient for all you may need to face. As we make joyful sounds about all of the above, our emotions will begin to settle and catch up with where our faith and confession are taking us.

Pray

Turn every anxious thought into prayer to Him. Do not let the thought hang around and convene any "what if" committee meetings in your head. Turn it immediately into prayer!

Give thanks

Thank Him for who He is, and for all that He has done in your life to date. Thank Him for His promises, thank Him that He will be there in your tomorrow.

Express trust in God

A powerful weapon against the demonspeak of anxiety is to continually verbalise the words, "Lord, I trust You for what is ahead."

> **Questions:** If the worst happens, will God still be God?
> Will He be there for you?
> Is He able to work for your good in everything?

Here are some strategies that anxiety employs, along with some associated thoughts. Look at these thoughts — these voices of anxiety — and come up with some GodSpeak to bring them into line.

Anxiety seeks to focus us on the future with an overly negative expectation, a future without the grace of God supplying all we need.

- "How are you going to possibly put up with this for the rest of your life?"
- "How will you possibly cope, if you haven't put enough away for your retirement?"
- "Your children are pretty naughty. If they continue this way they will get in real trouble as teenagers and end up in jail!"

Anxiety gets us looking forward in fear. It narrowly focuses us on all that could go wrong. It "awfulises" the potential wrong of tomorrow!

- "How on earth are you going to be able to afford that?"
- "What will happen to us?"
- "How will we cope?" (Note the fearful tone!)

Anxiety seeks to take God out of the picture.

Anxiety seeks to convince us that it is "irresponsible" not to worry!

Anxiety keeps us in our head, ignoring the assurance of God in our heart.

As followers of Jesus, our future is always hopeful, because Jesus is there with us.

Here are some powerful keys for taking anxiety captive and making it obey:

Take anxious thoughts captive early. Do not give anxiety "airtime" in your head. As soon as you are aware of an anxious thought coming, immediately begin to vocalise your trust in God, that He will be there in every situation, providing all you need for that situation.

Remember to note the tone and vocabulary of thoughts that come to you. Does this sound like a thought from heaven? Ask yourself where this line of thinking will take you: into peace and confidence, or into fear and anxiety?

Enlist help in the battle. Talk with someone about your thoughts; use that person as a sounding board. Have them pray with you and for you.

Develop the practice of rejoicing and giving thanks to God for His faithfulness. Begin your day with thanksgiving; end your day with rejoicing. Take opportunities during your day to give Him thanks and to vocalise your trust in Him and His provision, turning your focus to Him.

I love the story in 2 Chronicles chapter 20 where Jehoshaphat and his men were confronted with an overwhelming enemy army intent on their destruction. Their response was to pray a prayer that ended with this statement:

> *For we have no power to face this vast army that is attacking us. We do not know what to do, but our eyes are upon you.*
> 2 Chronicles 20:12

They acknowledged the seriousness of the situation and their own lack of power to overcome. They acknowledged that they did not know what to do. In the midst of all that, though, they powerfully acknowledge that their eyes — their attention — was on the Lord. My wife Lynda and I have often reminded each other of this verse and prayed it in tough situations we have faced.

Develop a lifestyle of committing everything to God in prayer, casting any anxiety on Him, because He cares for you. Again, do not give anxiety any "airtime" in your head. Immediately turn it into prayer and praise to Him.

Fill your mind with the scriptures; focus on God's faithfulness and power to work for good in everything. Find a way that works for you to regularly read and meditate on the scriptures.

Develop a picture in your mind and heart of a future with God's provision in it. Whatever happens tomorrow, God will be there with you, multiplying His amazing grace to you for any situation you face. Whenever you find yourself looking forward, train yourself to inject Christian hope into that future!

To help settle the physical effects of anxiety, *learn and practice relaxation breathing.* On every exhale, pray and give thanks. Also start doing some regular light to moderate aerobic exercise — it will really help.

Remember: Don't Worry! Be Prayerful!

> ***Reflection:*** In what areas does anxiety try to speak into your life?
> What is some GodSpeak you could apply to those areas?

DISCOURAGEMENT

I've had enough Lord!
Take my life!

1 Kings 19:4

Surely in vain I have kept my heart pure;
in vain have I washed my hands in innocence.
All day long I have been plagued;
I have been punished every morning.

Psalm 73:13-14

One of the ways the enemy seeks to "take us out" is through discouragement.

> *Then their enemies set out to discourage them and make them afraid to continue the work.*
> Ezra 4:4

The instruction to guard against discouragement is repeated many times in the opening chapters of Joshua.

> *Don't be terrified and don't be discouraged.*
> Joshua 1:9

Discouragement and fear often go hand in hand and feed off each other. Discouragement's other known associates are disappointment, self-pity, hopelessness, fatigue, and "the other person's grass is always greener".

Look at these two stories in the Bible of battles with discouragement.

The first is about Elijah. He had prophesied no rain on the nation, and it had undergone years of drought; he had seen miracle after miracle done at his hand and experienced daily miraculous provision. Elijah has just seen an outstanding demonstration of God's power, and a great victory over the prophets of Baal.

Now, in 1 Kings chapter 19, Elijah is running for his life. He seems to totally lose courage and slides into isolation ("I am the only righteous one left!") and deep depression, asking God to take his life.

The second is about Asaph, one of the writers of the Psalms. In Psalm 73 he recounts how he has become focused on the seeming success, popularity and comfort of people who are not following God. He has formed dark comparisons between their lives and his. His thinking has become so dark that he sees every moment of others' lives filled with joy and comfort, and every moment of his own life filled with torment. In the end he says to himself, "Living for God is a waste of time!" He goes on to say that when he tried to understand, it was oppressive to him. While he was in the dark place, he was senseless and ignorant.

These stories give us some useful insights into the strategies of discouragement. In Elijah's case, it came after major victory. We can often find ourselves in low times or times of anti-climax after a period of lots of exciting good things happening. Discouragement will seek to take advantage of us during these times.

As you read Asaph's story you can imagine he has had a string of disappointments, and they have built up and overcome him, leading to a total loss of perspective. We all suffer disappointments and setbacks. If we fail to deal with them adequately, they will build up and discouragement will ooze its way into our lives.

Carrying an unrealistic expectation that things will always go well will set us up for disappointment and discouragement. Carrying a religious belief that if we are "good" then God will totally shield us from all discomfort and hard times will also set us up for disappointment and discouragement.

Discouragement seeks to focus us on the negative things in our lives, eclipsing any appreciation of the aspects of our lives that are going well.

Discouragement gets us fixated on the negative things in our life. Asaph says, "All day long I have been plagued, I have been punished every morning."

Discouragement draws us into comparing ourselves with others. It exaggerates the negativity of our own life compared to the "wonderfulness" of others' lives.

Discouragement isolates us. In both Asaph's and Elijah's situations there is much use of the word "I": "I alone am left", "I am punished all day long."

Discouragement undermines our belief in the goodness of God. "Surely in vain I have kept my heart pure..." says Asaph. The same theme is found in the book of Malachi: "It is a waste of time living for God!"

Discouragement gives us a dark picture of our future.

The Voices of Discouragement

Discouragement sneaks in through self-pity.

- "You poor thing. You deserve better. It's just not fair."
- "No-one understands you."
- "Your wife doesn't appreciate you; she doesn't know how lucky she is."
- "This is just too hard."
- "The others really have it good."
- "Where is God when you really need Him?"
- "Those prayers have just not been answered."
- "It's just not fair. You deserve so much better."
- "After all you've done for them!"
- "Things are never going to change; just give up!"

Discouragement takes advantage of our low periods. When we are ill or fatigued, we can find ourselves more susceptible to discouragement. For some, like Elijah, the period immediately following a high time – like a great success or fun – can bring with it a feeling of anticlimax. This can leave us more susceptible to discouragement. Times of disappointment, grief and loss, if not adequately processed, can leave us more open to the voices of discouragement.

I struggled with discouragement in my own life for years. It would descend on me like a wet blanket, using voices of self-pity to get to me. One of my childhood memories is of being put to sleep by my grandmother stroking my hair and singing to me. When discouragement came to me, it would feel like that, like it was stroking my hair and saying things like: "You poor thing. It just isn't fair. You deserve better than this..." There was a strange sort of comfort and helplessness in it. The feeling was one of just curling up in a foetal position in the corner. This would leave me prone to all manner of temptation and false comforts.

One day I read of a woman who had struggled with being critical, and who felt challenged by God to go on a "criticism fast" — to allow no critical word to pass through her lips for a two-week period. This really impacted me, and I felt God speak to me about declaring a "discouragement fast" — a lifelong one! That day I declared war on discouragement and self-pity. That was a major turning point in my life. The old comforter was now my enemy! This meant recognising those first warm, familiar, anaesthetising feelings and thoughts of self-pity, and spurning their comforting embrace, denying myself the pleasure of their company. Resisting does not feel good at the time. However, it does get easier with time and practice. I am pleased to report that now, years down the track, discouragement is no longer part of my life. It is so good to live free of it!

Some Keys to Overcoming Discouragement

Declare war on discouragement
Make discouragement an enemy of your soul, rather than a "comforting" friend. Give yourself a real, solid foundation from which to regain your freedom.

Let go of unrealistic expectations
Discouragement is really just disappointments that have not been dealt with, that have festered into this all-encompassing "wet blanket" over our lives. The fact that we are wired to be people of hope, to be adventurous and try new things, means that some

times of failing and disappointment are inevitable — part of the human condition. Disappointment is linked to unfulfilled expectations. Therefore, it is really important to have realistic expectations, to develop a world view that says disappointment is part of the adventure, that it is normal and healthy to have some times of disappointment. This thinking helps us to develop good ways of dealing with disappointments, and to build emotional resilience. Jesus, before He left for heaven, equipped His disciples with a realistic expectation of hard times ahead for them. He then left them with these words:

> *I have told you these things, so that in me you may have peace. In this world you will have trouble. But take heart! I have overcome the world!*
> John 16:33

Jesus was seeking to build into these followers of His an emotional resilience based on realistic expectations and an ongoing connection with Him and His overcoming power.

Learn to recognise the voices of discouragement.

As you learn to apply some of the questions suggested in this book to the thoughts that come up in your mind, you will become more and more skilled at recognising demonspeak. You will become quicker at realising when you are being seduced and lulled into inactivity by strangely comforting thinking. There is a feeling and tone about the voices of discouragement that will become recognisable to you.

As soon as you recognise the voices of discouragement, take those thoughts captive! Don't give them time to take root in your mind and emotions. Remember, writing them down is a good way to take them captive. Immediately apply the truth to them; apply some scripture to them; apply some realistic expectation-based thinking to them. Make them obey Christ. Bring them into submission to Him and His amazing grace!

Learn to maintain hope in the Bible

The truth of the Bible has become a great strength in my life. Learn to live in the Word of God. Read it, think about it, quote it to yourself, write it down; do whatever works for you to make it a major part of your life and thinking! The scriptures are full of hope.

> *Sing to the Lord, you saints of His; praise His holy name.*
> *For His anger lasts only a moment, but His favour lasts a lifetime;*

> *Weeping may remain for a night but rejoicing comes in the morning.*
> Psalm 30:4-5

Hope says, "This is really tough now, but by His grace there is a time coming when I will be looking back on this. I will be through to the other side!"

Remember the word yet! I love this word. YET. It is a great hope word. I am not through this *yet*. My prayer has not been answered *yet*. I haven't seen the victory or breakthrough *yet*. I am not healed *yet*.

Look at what the prophet Habakkuk says.

> *Though the fig tree does not bud and there are no grapes on the vines,*
> *though the olive crop fails and the fields produce no food,*
> *though there are no sheep in the pen and no cattle in the stalls,*
> *yet I will rejoice in the Lord,*
> *I will be joyful in God my Saviour.*
> *The Sovereign Lord is my strength;*
> *He makes my feet like the feet of a deer,*
> *He enables me to go on the heights.*
> Habakkuk 3:17-19

Here we have the prophet using the word "yet" in another hope-filled way. He is saying that even though everything is currently a disaster, he is rejoicing in the Lord. He is being joyful in God his Saviour. He is looking past the circumstances, setting his gaze on the Lord who reigns. He is drawing strength from his God who will enable him to rise above the present dire circumstances.

Learn to refocus

Remember, discouragement uses harassment to keep us down; it narrows our focus right down onto the present negative circumstances. Regain a wider perspective through intentionally slowing down and taking time with the Lord. Take a bit of time to just be with Him. Pray, sing, give thanks, get into His Word. Learn to enjoy being "in the moment".

Learn to care for yourself

Learn to recognise the seasons of your life. If you are facing a really busy, emotionally and mentally taxing time ahead, then prepare for it by doing some things that refresh and replenish you. After really busy, tough, draining times, replenish again. If you have had a disappointing event or series of events, then do some journaling, or talk it through with someone and have them pray with you.

Take your disappointment to Jesus in prayer

Do not let disappointments pile up in your life without processing them, or they will fester and infect you. Learn ways that work for you to recoup emotionally, mentally and spiritually. Practise these regularly. Make sure you include in your lifestyle some aerobic exercise — it really helps. When discouragement seeks to have you curled up in self-pity, get yourself moving!

Learn to encourage yourself

An incident in David's life is a great example of a person encouraging himself. He and his men have returned to their hometown and find that it has been attacked and all their families have been kidnapped. They all weep aloud until they have no more tears. In their deep discouragement his men are talking of killing him!

> *David was greatly distressed because the men were talking of stoning him; each one was bitter in spirit because of his sons and daughters. But David found strength in the Lord his God.*
> 1 Samuel 30:6

David found strength in the Lord his God! I wonder how he did that? He was a musician, so maybe he did a bit of singing. Maybe he recounted to himself the times God had delivered him in the past. Maybe he remembered the lion and the bear. Maybe he remembered slaying Goliath. The point is, he knew how to find strength in God, to encourage himself. I know for myself that if I go and walk and pray for a period of time, I come back strengthened. There are some scriptures I can speak out and meditate on, and strength will come. I can get out my ukulele and sing to the Lord, and strength will come. For me, reminding myself of the call of God on my life and the aspects of that which are still ahead strengthens me.

David exercises some strong self-talk also.

> *Why are you downcast, O my soul?*
> *Why so disturbed within me?*
> *Put your hope in God, for I will yet praise Him,*
> *My Saviour and my God.*
> *My soul is downcast within me;*
> *therefore I will remember you.*
> Psalm 42: 5-6a

Here David is addressing his soul, his mind and emotions, telling them to focus on God his saviour. Notice the last phrase where he says that when he is down, he will remember his God. Notice that wonderful word "yet" word in these verses! Sometimes it is helpful for me to say out loud to myself, "Come on Graham, get up and into it; God is with you!"

Praise, thanksgiving and rejoicing

Work on becoming a champion in the areas of praise, thanksgiving and rejoicing. These activities powerfully focus us afresh on the goodness of God.

> *For the Lord takes delight in His people;*
> *He crowns the humble with salvation.*
> *Let the saints rejoice in this honour*
> *and sing for joy on their beds.*
> Psalm 149:4-5

Here we are encouraged to rejoice in the honour of being saved. How often do we meditate on how wonderful it is to belong to Jesus? In Luke 10:20 we are told to rejoice that our name is written in the Book of Life!

> *He who sacrifices thank offerings honours me,*
> *and he prepares the way*
> *so that I may show him the salvation of God.*
> Psalm 50:23

Here we are told that giving thanks honours God and prepares the way for His salvation.

Blessed are you when people insult you, persecute you and falsely say all kinds of evil against you because of me. Rejoice and be glad, because great is your reward in heaven, for in the same way they persecuted the prophets who were before you.
Matthew 5:11-12

Here we have one of those "realistic expectations" verses! Jesus is telling us to rejoice and be glad in the midst of persecution. I have recently been watching a video entitled *Sheep Among Wolves*, about the growing church in Iran. I was greatly impacted by a segment where a woman is talking about the persecution they live under. She says that she and her husband know that when they leave their house in the morning they may not return in the evening. If they are caught, they will be arrested, beaten, brutalised and killed. She then says that they have agreed together that they offer their bodies as a sacrifice to the Lord! They carry an expectation that their commitment to Jesus and His kingdom may mean death for them. Staying aware of the sufferings of our brothers and sisters globally keeps our expectations real. When we have realistic expectations and are practiced at rejoicing, we are strong against discouragement.

> *To provide for those who grieve in Zion,*
> *to bestow on them a crown of beauty instead*
> *of ashes,*
> *the oil of gladness instead of mourning,*
> *and a garment of praise instead of a spirit*
> *of despair.*
> *They will be called oaks of righteousness,*
> *a planting of the Lord*
> *for the display of His splendour.*
> Isaiah 61:3

This beautiful scripture lists the things God provides for us in place of discouragement. These are all available right now to you and me from the Holy Spirit. In the midst of this verse we see that He has given us a garment of praise that we can put on instead of a spirit of despair. The phrase "spirit of despair" is an apt description of discouragement. In times of despair, praise is something we can put on like a coat, by just beginning to voice praise to Him, and then continuing in it until our focus shifts to Jesus and what He has for us at this time. In the same way as we increase physical fitness by physical exercise, so we develop spiritual fitness and resilience by exercising these spiritual disciplines. As we do so, they become second nature to us, our "go to" places in times of trouble.

The psalmist finishes his story of losing and regaining perspective with these words:

*But as for me, it is good to be near God.
I have made the Sovereign Lord my refuge;
I will tell of all your deeds.*
Psalm 73:28

LET THERE BE JOY!

> ***Questions:*** What has stood out to you from this chapter?
> In what ways does discouragement affect your life?
> What would a declaration of war on discouragement look like to you?
> Which of the keys I mentioned above stand out to you?

A Footnote on Anger

Many of the scenarios above can push us into anger as well as discouragement. There are screeds of writing out there on this subject, but I have found the *Telling Yourself the Truth* series by William Backus particularly informative and helpful.

If your struggle is with anger, I wonder what demonspeak operates in your mind. I wonder what old tracks are continually playing in your head. The well-known one in the field of domestic violence is, "If she would just shut her mouth, I wouldn't hit her!" Demonspeak always places the responsibility for our behaviour on others, often the victims of our outpourings.

There is a region north of where I live that would consistently flood when there was any significant rainfall at all. That is because it was by a river in the midst of a peat swamp. The water table was always high and so it only needed a small amount of added water to cause it to flood. Nowadays, the swamp has been drained and buildings have gone up on it. It is far less prone to flooding.

Many of us have a very high anger water table, so fairly insignificant events can cause our anger to flood over others around us. Demonspeak seeks to deflect us from examining and understanding what keeps that water table so high by placing the blame on others. The enemy will do what he can to keep us from draining that swamp and getting some useful building done in our lives.

Discouragement

Having unrealistic expectations that go unmet will raise that water table. Not dealing with disappointment will raise the water table. So, will not dealing with that "unbearable feeling" of being disagreed with, of being told no to something you really want, of feeling ridiculed or disrespected, of not being in control of what is happening, of being wrong over an issue. Maybe there are themes like "life is not fair", or "nothing good ever happens to me" going on there. While these may feel really uncomfortable, they are no excuse for angry outpourings.

As I think of the tantrums I have personally thrown, they were always right out of proportion to whatever the precipitating event was and were fuelled by a build-up of events that caused discomfort, frustration and/or disappointment.

Doing some journaling of the angry event and reflecting on the thoughts involved and the lead up to the outburst will often yield valuable insights into ways of breaking the cycle of anger build up and associated demonspeak.

Our *Liberation Manual* tells us that our anger does not bring about godly results, that it will mock us. It tells us to not let anger cause us to sin.

In my work with couples, I have seen just how destructive the outpouring of anger is to real intimacy. It just kills it. I have also seen how it whittles away at the good will in a relationship. Our anger shuts our loved ones' hearts down toward us.

Decide today to do the work necessary to overcome in this area. Freedom and healed, revitalised relationships await you.

MISSION

Who am I that I should go?
I cannot speak well.
Please send someone else.

Exodus 3:11 and 4:13

(My paraphrase)

When Jesus left this earth, He left us a task to complete. That task is known as The Great Commission.

> *After Jesus rose from the dead, He told them to go to a mountain in Galilee and He would meet them there. When they saw Him, they worshiped Him; but some doubted. Then Jesus came to them and said, "All authority in heaven and on earth has been given to me. Therefore, go and make disciples of all nations, baptising them in the name of the Father and of the Son and of the Holy Spirit, and teaching them to obey everything I have commanded you. And surely I am with you always, to the very end of the age."*
> Matthew 28:17-20

I am amazed when I read that, in this awesome encounter with the risen Christ, some of the disciples still doubted. This Great Commission was given to some pretty ordinary people who had some struggles.

For the past three decades I have been leading among ordinary people who have decided to make Jesus' command their first priority. We have prayed, inspired one another, mobilised and sent people as workers to the nations. During that time, we have seen a couple of million dollars released into this great cause.

We have also involved ourselves in the ongoing support and encouragement of those on the field.

As part of this, one of the amazing privileges Lynda and I have is visiting and supporting cross-cultural workers on the field. As we have sat with various ones of these folks, I have observed very similar struggles and forms of demonspeak that seek to bring these amazing people down and take them out of their place in the purposes of God. These same struggles are faced by those of us who send and support them. They are present whenever we set out to accomplish things in God, regardless of our location.

The enemy is heavily invested in keeping us from truly rising up and fully obeying Jesus.

In the account of the rebuilding of the walls of Jerusalem in the book of Nehemiah, we see some excellent exposés of the ploys the enemy uses against the people of God to try to keep them from the great work He has given them to do. While the book of Nehemiah is the account of God's people involved in a great work — the rebuilding of the wall — we also are involved in THE great work — the Great Commission:

seeing the good news of the gospel going to everyone everywhere, and seeing His kingdom come and His will be done on earth as in heaven. This is the ultimate team sport. We're in it together!

> *"Everyone who calls on the name of The Lord will be saved." How then can they call on the one they have not believed in? And how can they believe in the one of whom they have not heard? And how can they hear without someone preaching to them? And how can they preach unless they are sent? As it is written, "How beautiful are the feet of them that bring good news!"*
>
> Romans 10:13-15

In the subsections below, let's look at the ploys of the enemy that are described in Nehemiah. These give us valuable insights both for praying for our overseas workers, and for being prepared for the attacks of the enemy on our own involvement in God's purposes.

Ridicule

> *What are these feeble Jews doing? Will they restore their wall? Will they offer sacrifices? Will they finish in a day? Can they bring the stones*

back to life from those heaps of rubble — burned as they are? What they are building — if even a fox climbed up onto it, he would break down their wall of stones!
Nehemiah 4:2-3

Here we have the enemy ridiculing the people of God, pouring scorn on them. This is a boringly regular ploy of the enemy. It has the theme of "Who do you think you are?"

As we sit with overseas workers, we often hear the accusing voices of ridicule: "You're so ordinary! What a failure! You're not doing anything worthwhile. You might as well have stayed home. What a fraud!"

As we at home seek to serve as senders by committing to give financially through self-sacrifice and believing God for His supply, by praying and encouraging, we often encounter ridicule: "Who do you think you are? Change the world, impact nations — what a joke! What difference is your few dollars going to make? God supplying? So, when and where is that going to happen? You can hardly make ends meet yourself!"

As we seek to live intentional lives towards people in our own world who have yet to connect with Jesus, praying for them and taking opportunities to tell of and demonstrate the love of Christ, we will face similar ridicule: "As if you can make a difference in people's lives! You are such a pathetic Christian yourself, why would anyone else want to follow Jesus? What a joke!"

As we respond to an idea or vision God has given us that will do good in Jesus' name, we will often face similar voices. The enemy is continually seeking to attack our sense of competency, our sense of self. Learn to recognise these thoughts as utter demonspeak (and therefore lies), take them captive, and make them obey Christ. This is the enemy reacting to you pursuing the purposes of God! Apply the truth to the situation.

> *But you will receive power when the Holy Spirit comes on you; and you will be my witnesses in Jerusalem, and in all Judea and Samaria, and to the ends of the earth.*
> Acts 1:8

> *Such confidence as this is ours through Christ before God. Not that we are competent in ourselves to claim anything for ourselves, but our competence comes from God. He has made us competent as ministers of a new covenant — not of the letter but of the Spirit; for the letter kills, but the Spirit gives life.*
> 2 Corinthians 3:4-6

> *But by the grace of God I am what I am, and His grace to me was not without effect.*
>
> 1 Corinthians 15:10a

The truth is that, when God calls us deeper into His purposes, He equips. He provides everything we need for that which He calls us to. It is all by His grace and enabling!

Discouragement

> *The strength of the labourers is giving out, and there is so much rubble we cannot rebuild the wall.*
>
> Nehemiah 4: 10

Here we see that fatigue is setting in, and the enormity of the task is becoming overwhelming for the people. You can pretty much guarantee that, before you accomplish what God has given you to do, you will face fatigue and be attacked by the voices of discouragement. To use a golfing term, it is par for the course.

As we sit with our overseas workers, we hear the same old demonspeak. "You're never going to get the language. If those supporters back home knew how ineffective you are, they would stop supporting you.

What a waste of money. You should be doing much better than this!"

As supporting senders, we will face similar attacking thoughts. "You haven't seen much money come in yet for your mission faith commitment... and your car broke down. How come? So much for God multiplying back to you. You knew it wouldn't really work, not for you!"

As we seek to invest in the lives of the people in our world, we will face some rejections, "slaps in the face" and disappointments. The demonspeak of discouragement will seek to take advantage of those situations.

Refer back to the chapter on discouragement for overcoming this.

Intimidation

> *Also, our enemies said, "Before they know it or see us, we will be right there among them and will kill them and put an end to the work." Then the Jews who lived near them came and told us ten times over, "Wherever you turn, they will attack us."*
> Nehemiah 4:11-12

Our folks overseas, particularly those in closed countries, face all sorts of intimidating thoughts and voices. "The authorities will discover what you are doing. It's OK for you, you will just get sent home, but what about the locals you work with? They'll do long terms in jail! Should you really be putting them at risk like that? Is this really God's will?" They also face tormenting thoughts of what will happen if they or their children get seriously injured or ill.

As senders, we will face our own demonspeak. "This extra giving is going to mess up your finances; people are going to think you are unwise. Imagine what you could have done with the money you've already given!"

As we seek to reach out in our world, we will face the demonspeak of intimidation: "These people will think you are an idiot. You will be the reject, the laughingstock of your school or workplace. You will probably turn them off following Jesus forever. They will ask questions you don't have the answers to."

Look back over the chapter on anxiety for insights into overcoming intimidation.

Disunity

Now the men and their wives raised a great outcry against their Jewish brothers!
Nehemiah 5:1

A major reason for overseas workers returning early from the field is relationship difficulties with others on their team. It is a real battle on the field, as a diverse collection of people are brought together in God's purposes. They are all facing the pressures of being in a culture that is not their own, and generally they are under quite a bit of stress.

The enemy hates unity. When we are working in unity towards a common purpose, it is an awesome thing. The enemy will do what he can to divide us.

Be aware of this enemy tactic, and quickly take captive any thoughts that are spoiling your attitude towards your fellow workers. Know that the enemy is heavily invested in magnifying every little offence. If you have got "buttons", you can be sure they will be pressed. Operate in the opposite spirit to disunity and division. Learn to keep short accounts with others. Always apply the best possible interpretation to other people's words and actions. Practice forgiveness, speak blessing, and intercede for the ones with whom you are working.

Mission

Look at what Paul writes to the early Christians in Colossae and Ephesus:

Bear with each other and forgive whatever grievances you may have against one another. Forgive as the Lord forgave you. And over all these virtues put on love, which binds them all together in perfect unity. Let the peace of Christ rule in your hearts, since as members of one body you were called to peace. And be thankful.
Colossians 3:13-15

Be completely humble and gentle; be patient, bearing with one another in love. Make every effort to keep the unity of the Spirit through the bond of peace.
Ephesians 4:2-3

The scriptures assume there will be challenges to our unity and so gives these specific instructions.

Distraction

"Let us meet together in one of the villages on the plain of Ono. I am carrying on a great work and cannot go down..."

"Why should I stop work while I leave and go down to you?" Four times they sent me the same

> *message, and each time I gave them the same answer.*
>
> Nehemiah 6:2-4

Sometimes folks on the overseas mission field can feel like they are totally consumed with the business of just living day to day in another culture, with little language and inadequate support structures. Sometimes it seems that all their energy is used up dealing with relational issues. Then there are the "opportunities" that come and deflect them from their main purpose.

I reflect on my own life, and even on getting this book completed. The number of times I have sat down to work on it, and had my mind assailed by a tumult of other things that need doing, or I find myself drawn to some silly game on the computer. Procrastination, sloth's first cousin, uses distraction to keep us from our main purpose. Add to this the constant clamour of toys, entertainment, and the "shoulds" of our society, and opportunities for distraction abound!

A good question to ask in these situations might be, "Is this thought taking me into accomplishing what I have set out to do?" You will find yourself becoming more and more aware of the thoughts that come into your mind, and this will give you the opportunity to take them captive.

Temptation to Sin

> *"Let us meet in the house of God, inside the temple, and let us close the temple doors, because men are coming to kill you – by night they are coming to kill you."*
> *But I said, "Should a man like me run away? Or should one like me go into the temple to save his life? I will not go!" I realised that God had not sent him, but that he had prophesied against me, because Tobiah and Sanbballat had hired him. He had been hired to intimidate me so that I would commit a sin by doing this, and then they would give me a bad name to discredit me.*
> Nehemiah 6:10-13

Like the rest of us, our overseas workers have areas of weakness that they are working on. The enemy will put all the pressure he can on us. He loves it when a number of stressors coincide, forming a "perfect storm" in our lives. It is during these times that he seeks to lure us into sin, and to then discredit and disqualify us.

Knowing this ploy of the enemy, let's do all we can to keep sharp. Spend time with people who build you up and keep you focussed. Develop excellent accountability relationships.

We are co-workers with God, with our leaders, with our missionaries, and with each other. Let's co-operate together for THE great task. Pray for our workers overseas, our leaders and each other: "Keep us from temptation; keep us sharp; protect us body, soul, and spirit!" Pray continually over your missions giving, that God would provide, multiply its use, and multiply it back to you as further seed for sowing.

> *So do not throw away your confidence; it will be richly rewarded. You need to persevere so that when you have done the will of God, you will receive what He has promised.*
> Hebrews 10:35-36

Questions: What has stood out to you from this chapter?
Which strategies do you see the enemy has used to stop you moving forward in God's purposes?

TEMPTATION AND SIN

Sin is crouching at your door;
it desires to have you, but you must master it.

Genesis 4:7b

In the beginning of the third chapter of Genesis we have the account of sin's entry into humanity. We read that the devil basically told Eve that God was lying to her, withholding a good thing from her that would enrich her life. In an unimaginably perfect orchard full of all kinds of delightful things to sample, the "forbidden fruit" of that particular tree suddenly became very attractive.

In the gospel of John, we are told that the devil is a liar who is committed to our absolute poverty and destruction.

I am a keen salt-water fisherman. When I go after a large snapper, I do not put down a big, highly visible hook with a note in snapper language announcing that I am here to catch, kill and eat him! Instead, I get some of the food that he particularly likes, and I wrap it around a hook and quietly drop it into the water, hoping the snapper will be so enticed by the bait that he doesn't notice the hook and just gulps it down.

Sin is like that. It appears desirable but is full of hooks! In the cold light of day, though, we know that sin is not good for us, our family, or society in general.

Here is the Bible's exposé on sin:

> *When tempted, no one should say, "God is tempting me." For God cannot be tempted by evil, nor does He tempt anyone; but each one is tempted when, by his own evil desire, he is dragged away and enticed. Then, after desire has conceived, it gives birth to sin; and sin, when it is full-grown, gives birth to death.*
> James 1:13-15

Sin Makes Use of the Temptation Process

From the verses above, we can see the progression of temptation:

> We are dragged away and enticed by our own evil desires.

> That evil desire conceives and gives birth to a sinful action.

> Fully-grown sin becomes death.

Suppose, for example, that I as a married man have a co-worker who I find incredibly attractive. She is warm and outgoing, and very affirming of me. My marriage, meanwhile, is in one of those tired phases and there is not much of anything going on at home. The thought comes (from you know where!), "It would be much better to be with her; she appreciates you and affirms you." What I do with that initial thought is so important. If I entertain the thought and maybe begin to fantasise about what it would be like to be with my co-worker instead of my wife, then I have engaged in the temptation process. Those thoughts will give birth to other thoughts, to plans of action, and to the action itself, bringing a load of hurt with it!

The time to deal with temptation is when it first comes in thought form. In Malachi 2:15, men are told to "guard themselves in their spirit" and thus to not break faith with the wife of their youth. It all begins with a seed thought. So I treat those feelings of attraction and those seducing thoughts as the demonspeak that they are, and deal with them immediately. I replace them with statements of scripture, declaring myself a son of God, a man who is called to delight myself in the wife of my youth (Proverbs 5:18) and to love her as Christ loved the church and gave Himself for it (Ephesians 5:25). I once heard it said that sin destroys, and your sin will destroy you and your loved ones; we are told in Romans 7:11 and Romans 6:23 that sin brings death. I remind myself of the nature of sin and its consequences on my loved ones and myself.

Sin is Opportunistic

For sin, seizing the opportunity afforded by the commandment, deceived me, and through the commandment put me to death.

Romans 7:11

There are certain situations in which we are more prone to temptation than others. I understand that addicts are sometimes taught the acronym HALT to help them be aware of when they are more likely to be drawn back into addiction. I have added an S.

Hungry

Angry

Lonely

Tired

Sad

To this list we could add times when we are bored, or times of anticlimax just after a period of great excitement or accomplishment. I wonder what other conditions might set you up for temptation? When working with people who struggle with persistent temptation in certain areas, I often find that it is at certain times of the day that they are more susceptible than at other times.

I remember one therapist who would work with people to identify what he called their "unbearable feeling": that feeling that is extremely stressful for us, that sets us up for temptation and sin. It may be feeling unappreciated, misunderstood, not in control, not listened to, or not being able to instantly have what you desperately want, or feeling like you are being looked down on or laughed at. These are situations of discomfort that set us up for some old, familiar false comforter.

As we understand the strategies of temptation and what goes on for us, we can arm ourselves against it.

Sin Deceives

Let's look at some common demonspeak of sin attempting to deceive us, and our potential responses based on God's Word.

- "This will be exciting, good for you! You are missing out."

In Romans 6:23 I read that the wages of sin is death, and it says in John 10:10 that you, devil, come to rob, kill and destroy. It is Jesus who gives life in its fullness.

Temptation and Sin

- "You deserve this! It's time for some fun, some pleasure!"

I am not my own, I was bought at a price. I will therefore glorify God with my Body! (1 Corinthians 6:20)

I am embracing not having what I really want. This is training me! (Hebrews 12:7)

- "No-one will ever know!"

Be sure your sin will find you out! (Numbers 32:23)

- "Just this once, it will be OK."

By nature, sin wants to have me; it has hooks! (Genesis 4:7) I have learned about the "hooks" in temptation, and this one is full of them!

- "Remember how good it was when...?"

Those things didn't benefit me, and I am now ashamed of them; they result in death! (Romans 6: 21)

- "You can't resist; this is too strong for you."

Heaps of Christians have overcome this, I have overcome other things, and in this temptation, God has provided a way out. I'll see it soon, and this will be yet another overcome sin in my life. (1 Corinthians 10:13)

- "You've blown it now! God won't help you. You might as well keep doing it!"

No! I confess my sins, and God is faithful and just to forgive me and make me clean from all unrighteousness. This sin is on borrowed time! (1 John 1:9)

- "Go on, God will forgive you!"

No way! I know the plans that sin has for my life! I am absolutely blown away by God's forgiveness. It causes me to respect and love Him, not to presume upon Him! (Psalm 130:4, 1 John 2:1)

- "You know how sinful you and your ancestors have been; you are not going to change!"

I am forgiven. I am redeemed and set free from the empty ways of living handed down to me from my forefathers. (1 Peter 1:18-19).

God will complete the work He has started in me! (Philippians 1:6)

My whole spirit, soul and body will be blameless at His coming. (1 Thessalonians 5:23-24)

Graham told me that when some demon reminds me of my past, I should remind him of his future!

> ***Questions:*** What other examples of demonspeak can you think of, and what scriptural truth can you fire at them?
>
> What areas of demonspeak do you recognise in your own life, and what are the relevant truths to be applied?

Some Thoughts for Those Breaking Free from Addiction

When we feel drawn back into old addictive practices, it is often a combination of things, a "perfect storm" if you like. A situation arises that brings some kind of discomfort. We start to experience the old hunger or longing. This is accompanied by the whisperings of an old familiar demon, and we find ourselves back into it. Our task is to decline the invitations of that old familiar spirit, and to listen instead for the promptings of the Holy Spirit. We can meet those whisperings with immediate worship to Jesus, and immediately vocalise our love and desire for more of the voice of the Holy Spirit in our lives.

The answer to our addictions — and indeed to every temptation — is devotion to Jesus. As we fall more in love with Him, that replaces our love of addiction, false comfort and sin.

Receiving His ongoing forgiveness and cleansing

A powerful key to overcoming temptation and sin is by constantly applying the following verse to our lives:

> *If we confess our sins, He is faithful and just and will forgive us our sins and purify us from all unrighteousness.*
> 1 John 1:9

We are told here that if we sin, we are to confess our sin to God, and He will forgive us. Notice it does not say anything about feeling truly sorry or promising never to do that again. It does not talk about begging God to forgive you. It simply says to confess your sin to Him, and He will definitely forgive you your sin. Forgiveness is there waiting for you and me to receive from Him!

But wait, there's more...

God also promises to purify us from all unrighteousness. As I read this, I picture myself coming to God with dirty hands, and He forgives me and washes my hands. Then He says, "While you are here, I will give you a bath as well." Every time we confess our sin and receive His forgiveness, we are cleansed at a deeper and deeper level from things we are not even aware of yet.

The enemy will come and try to convince us that we have used all our chances with God. The truth is that His forgiveness is constantly there for us, activated by us coming to Him and confessing to Him. As mentioned earlier, I have often been asked, "Just how many times can I come to God over the same sin?" My answer is, "As often as it takes for you to grow so in love with Jesus that you no longer go to the old familiar behaviour; as many times as you need to discover the way to overcome in that area of your life." We are promised that, with every temptation, God provides a way for us to overcome it.

> *No temptation has seized you except what is common to man. And God is faithful; He will not let you be tempted beyond what you can bear. But when you are tempted, He will also provide a way out so that you can stand up under it.*
> 1 Corinthians 10:13

demonSPEAK

> ***Questions:*** What times of the day or days of the week are you more open to temptation?
> What situation arises to set you up?
> What is it that keeps tripping you up?
> What it is that sets you up for another relapse?
> Is it self-pity? Boredom? A feeling of "it's not fair?"
> Is it falling out with others and "spitting the dummy"?
> Identify your "unbearable feeling" and learn to sit with it, rather than self-medicate with it. For instance, it is normal and healthy to sometimes feel sad or angry, so what else could you do when you feel your "unbearable feeling" that is not sinful?

Hang in there! You are going to make it!

May God Himself, the God of peace, sanctify you through and through. May your whole spirit, soul and body be kept blameless at the coming of our Lord Jesus Christ. The one who calls you is faithful, and He will do it!
1 Thessalonians 5:23-24

SUFFERING

I consider that our present sufferings
are not worth comparing
with the glory that will be revealed in us.

Romans 8:18

demonSPEAK

One of the privileges afforded to me as a pastor and counsellor is the experience of being with people in the extreme times of their lives: rejoicing with them in the wonderful times of marriage, the birth of a child, miracles of healing; walking with them through the dark times of grief and suffering, of unanswered questions and unanswered prayers.

Sometimes things just don't make sense; there seems no rhyme or reason as to why things happen. The great apostle Paul, when confronted with situations he could not understand, writes in 2 Corinthians 4:8 of being perplexed but not in despair. Likewise, Asaph, the writer of Psalm 73, says that when he tried to understand the situation that confronted him, it was oppressive to him. Yet through encounters with God he was able to make sense of it, and he finishes the psalm by saying that it is good to be near God and that he would tell of His works.

I know a man who went as a missionary to an unreached jungle tribe in Irian Jaya. He was only there for a short while when he became really ill and had to be evacuated. He recovered and returned to the tribe. He soon fell ill again and was evacuated before returning yet again. This happened several more times. You can imagine the questions that must have been going through his mind. It would have been easy to get discouraged in the middle of this suffering. Eventually though, the missionary ended up seeing real breakthrough in this tribe, with virtually the whole village coming to Christ. They reported to him later that when he first arrived and got ill so quickly, they thought that he would not be back. But when they observed him continually returning, they figured that what he had to say to them must be really important! His suffering created an opening for the gospel.

Many people of my generation know of Corrie Ten Boom, a Dutch lady who survived the horrors of a Nazi concentration camp, and later became a veritable "apostle of forgiveness" as she shared her experiences of coming to a place of being able, with God's help, to forgive the people who had committed atrocities against her and her family members. She took her story and its message of forgiving our enemies around the world, bringing release and healing to many.

Then there is the story in the *Liberation Manual* of Joseph, the youngest and favourite son in his family. His brothers grow to resent and hate him, and while he is still a teenager, they take the opportunity to sell him into slavery. He becomes a slave in Potiphar's house and, because the favour of God is on him, he becomes second in charge of the household. After many attempts at seducing him, Potiphar's wife falsely accuses him of sexual assault, and he is thrown in prison. Imagine the sense of rejection and injustice that would have assailed him. However, the favour of God is with him there also, and he is entrusted with much of the running of the prison. He is then called upon to interpret a dream that Pharaoh has had, does so and finds himself elevated to second in charge of the nation of Egypt. In the end he is reunited with his brothers and father. His brothers are fearful of what he might do, but his words to them are, "What you planned for evil, God worked for good to the saving of many lives." (Genesis 50:20) Instead of revenge, Joseph had powerful insight into the hand of God working through his suffering.

Suffering and hard times are pretty much part of the human experience. As we get a global picture of our planet and what goes on every day, we see that it is an incredibly unjust and difficult place for many.

When we face our own "dark nights of the soul" — our own times of suffering — the enemy will try to create an opportunity to torment us and bring us down. It is a tactical opportunity for him.

Here are some examples of demonspeak in our times of suffering:

- "You're suffering, so there must be something really wrong with you."
- "God is punishing you."
- "Does God REALLY love you? He doesn't seem to be answering your prayers." (Remember the YET word!)
- "What a waste of time it is serving God!" (Malachi 3:14-15, Psalm 73:13-15.)
- "God's not real."
- "You don't have enough faith."
- "There must be sin in your life that's stopping God answering!"
- "You're not good enough for God to come through for you!"
- "Why, why, why?!"

Remember, the enemy seeks to undermine our ideas of God's goodness, love and very existence. He is also intent on eroding our sense of self. He torments, goads, and seeks to wear us down.

Our *Liberation Manual* gives us many resources against the enemy for our times of suffering, such as these:

In Isaiah 63:9 we are told that in all our distress he is distressed, His presence saves us, His love and mercy redeem us, and He lifts us up and carries us.

In Genesis 50:20 we have Joseph's words that what the enemy planned for evil, God worked for good to the saving of many souls.

In Romans 8:28 we have the wonderful words that in all things God works for the good of those who love Him and are called by Him.

In 2 Corinthians 1:3 we have the God of all comfort who comforts us in all our distress so that we may comfort others with the comfort we have received.

The apostle Peter tells us in 1 Peter 4:19 that in our suffering we should commit ourselves to our faithful Creator and continue to do good.

The overwhelming message of the Bible is that God is with us. One of the Old Testament names of God is Jehovah Shammah: The God Who is There. One of the names of Jesus, Emmanuel, means exactly that: God is with us. Even when we don't feel His presence, He is there.

You may be familiar with the following well-known poem, of unknown authorship, which talks about God's presence with us during the most difficult times of our lives.

Footprints

One night I dreamed a dream.
As I was walking along the beach with my Lord.
Across the dark sky flashed scenes from my life.
For each scene, I noticed two sets of footprints in the sand, One belonging to me and one to my Lord.

After the last scene of my life flashed before me,
I looked back at the footprints in the sand.
I noticed that at many times along the path of my life,
especially at the very lowest and saddest times,
there was only one set of footprints.

This really troubled me, so I asked the Lord about it.
"Lord, you said once I decided to follow you,
You'd walk with me all the way.
But I noticed that during the saddest and most troublesome times of my life,

> *there was only one set of footprints.*
> *I don't understand why, when I needed You the most,*
> *You would leave me."*
>
> *He whispered, "My precious child,*
> *I love you and will never leave you.*
> *During your times of trial and suffering*
> *when you saw only one set of footprints,*
> *it was then that I carried you."*

Don't be surprised when the suffering in the world touches your life! During your times of suffering, though, don't allow demonspeak to drive a rift between you and God. He is your source of comfort and help!

Reflection: What has stood out to you from this chapter?
Are there ways the enemy has affected your trust in God through your own times of suffering?
What might you put into action to help you?

LIGHT AND DARKNESS

This is the message we have heard from Him
and declare to you: God is light;
in Him there is no darkness at all.

1 John 1:5

The enemy is referred to as the prince of darkness, and where he rules is called the dominion of darkness. In contrast to this, one of the names that God has made Himself known by is Light, and Jesus' kingdom is the Kingdom of Light. In 1 John 1:5 we are told that God is light and in Him there is no darkness at all. Hebrews 4:12-13 tells us that nothing in all creation is hidden from God's sight; everything is open and laid bare before His eyes. It tells us that His Word searches and judges our thoughts, attitudes and motivations. Jesus is referred to in John 1:9 as the true light that gives light to every person. He knows us through and through, and loves and embraces us. Amazing grace!

> *But if we walk in the light, as He is in the light, we have fellowship with one another, and the blood of Jesus, His Son, purifies us from all sin.*
> 1 John 1:7

God calls us to walk in the light as He is in the light, to come into the light, into transparency and openness. Someone has said that the power of sin is in its secrecy. We all live with a fear of exposure. While it is healthy and appropriate to have boundaries and privacy, it becomes problematic when we spend our life hiding. I am sure that we all sit around at times convinced that no one is as messed up as we are and making sure that no one gets a glimpse of our real internal world. The enemy loves to hold us there, hidden in the dark.

Look at what the gospel of John says:

> *This is the verdict: Light has come into the world, but men loved darkness instead of light because their deeds were evil. Everyone who does evil hates the light and will not come into the light for fear that his deeds will be exposed. But whoever lives by the truth comes into the light, so that it may be seen plainly that what he has done has been done through God.*
> John 3:19-21

You and I need to be absolutely open and transparent before God. He knows it all anyway. Then we need to take the brave step of having others in our life that we can be open and transparent with, people who love us and have shown themselves trustworthy. The enemy will do everything he can to keep us hiding in the shadows.

> *He who conceals his sins does not prosper, but whoever confesses and renounces them finds mercy.*
>
> Proverbs 28:13
>
> (Also check out Psalm 32:3-5)

In James 5:16 we are told to confess our sins to one another and pray for one another so we will be healed. Our prayers are powerful and effective.

In Ephesians 5:8 we are told that we were once darkness but now we are light in the Lord. Therefore, we are to live as children of light.

From the beginning of human experience, sin has led to hiddenness, with Adam and Eve hiding from God after they ate the forbidden fruit. As followers of Jesus, we are called into the light.

The enemy's primary weapon to keep us in darkness is shame. He uses thoughts like:

- "What will they think? They will reject you!"
- "No-one else in the church struggles with this!"
- "Telling the truth is too costly!"
- "Stay hidden, it is safer!"

Reject these thoughts! Arm yourself with the scriptures above and step into the light!

Come to the light! It is where freedom is!

> ***Reflection:*** What areas of your life do you need to (wisely) bring into the light?
> What people are there in your life that have shown themselves trustworthy?
> What might your first steps into the light look like?

MARRIAGE AND RELATIONSHIPS

Delight yourself in your marriage partner.
Be always satisfied by them.
Always be captivated by them.

Proverbs 5:18-19

(My own paraphrase)

One of the many enjoyable parts of my experience as a pastor has been officiating in probably hundreds of people's marriages and taking couples through pre-marriage counselling beforehand. I have yet to sit down with a couple and hear them tell me that they are planning to marry, live together while growing apart, and then hurt each other through a painful divorce. Yet this happens all too often! Stuff happens, the rot sets in, and before you know it these very "in love" people are feeling anything but love towards each other. This is a testimony to demonspeak. I believe most marriages break down because of "seeds of destruction" that were brought into the marriage by one or both partners. These may be unrealistic expectations, addictions (pornography is a growing issue here), insecurities, reactions based on broken parental or past relationships... the list is long and extensive. It is these things that demonspeak takes advantage of.

I have been married to Lynda for forty-eight years at the time of writing this. She is still the person I most want with me to share new experiences. I still love what I see when I look at her. I admire and respect so much about who she is and the giftings she carries.

Marriage and Relationships

Yet we are very different people. I was a surfer when we met, and Lynda still does not swim. I was an outrageously loud extrovert. She was much less so. Our primary "love languages" are quite different.

My dad was married several times and had some other relationships as well. Lifelong faithful marriage was not well modelled to me.

These factors provided plenty of ammunition and fertile ground for demonspeak! In the times when things got a bit dark between us (those times are pretty much guaranteed in long-term relationships) I would have this voice very clearly in my head saying, "You are just like your father; leave her!" That thought would come with accompanying feelings. Recognising it for what it was, I was able to take this thought captive, and declare God's truth over my life and marriage: "In this regard, I am not my earthly father's son. I am my Heavenly Father's son. His love and faithfulness run through my veins! I recommit myself to be His son, and the husband Lynda needs and deserves. In Jesus' name!"

I remember reading the book *Things We Wish We Had Said* by Tony Campolo and his adult son Bart. It is basically a number of letters written to each other about life. In writing about marriage, Tony says that there were times in his marriage which could have led to divorce, but he and his wife did not consider that to be an option for them. Then he makes a statement something like this: "By doing for each other what lovers are supposed to do for each other, even when we didn't feel like it, we eventually experienced the resurrection of what had been killed; what came to life again always seemed richer and deeper than what we had before." I love that phrase: "doing the things lovers are supposed to do for each other." It is so free of emotion; it is a statement of doing. Demonspeak will seek to take advantage of our feelings, our low, dark times. Remember, feelings come and go and will respond to continued healthy action.

Demonspeak will attack us in our times of feeling distant, neglected, misunderstood, unloved, or hurt. The enemy may not be as direct with you as he was with my "You're just like your father" attack but attack he will. There may be thoughts of comparison with past relationships, or with another person that you might have married. Maybe it will be thoughts of "I wonder how much better off you'd be if you were married to this person that you are beginning to feel attracted to?" It will probably include some "You deserve better than this" self-pity thoughts. There may also be some physical comparisons between your partner and someone else you are noticing.

You can be sure of one thing: these thoughts will be taking you down the pathway of destruction of your relationship. They will be filling you with hopelessness about the future of your marriage. They will be malevolent and insidious. The enemy hates committed, loving relationships and strong homes.

Solomon writes to a male readership in Proverbs chapter five (my paraphrase):

> *Let your fountain be blessed. Delight yourself in the wife of your youth. Let her breasts satisfy you always. Be intoxicated with her love. Why be intoxicated by an adulterous relationship? Why embrace the bosom of another man's wife? The Lord sees our ways. He examines all our paths.*

These are pretty erotic words from the Bible! God's truth calls us to let our ability to be sexual be a blessing, to delight ourselves in our marriage partner, to be satisfied always with how they are physically. It is a call to focus. Let them be at the center of your romantic and erotic fantasies. Be intoxicated with what you have, and do not be drawn off into the world of adultery. God's truth reminds us that the Lord sees and is there with His amazing grace to help us.

Remember, Malachi 2:15 tells us to guard ourselves in our spirits and not be unfaithful to our marriage partner. Unfaithfulness starts off with a poisonous seed of demonspeak, some little thought of self-pity, resentment, or hopelessness. That thought, if not taken captive, will fester and grow, bringing destruction to you and your relationships.

Every thought that seeks to take us away from that focus on our partner is demonspeak. I often tell people that getting married was once referred to as going to the altar together. An altar is where things are killed and sacrificed. When we enter into marriage, we are declaring ourselves dead to any romantic, erotic relationship with anyone but the one we are marrying, for the rest of our lives.

Demonspeak gets our focus on ourselves, what we want and need. God focuses us on His purpose and plan for our marriage: to be a witness to the world of Christ's love for His church, a visible demonstration to those around us of what love looks like, and a stable platform for our children and grandchildren to launch into their lives from.

When I begin to feel distance or resentment trying to seep into our marriage, I treat that as a signal to verbalise more strongly my love for Lynda and my commitment to her, a signal to begin calling down the blessing of God on her life, standing against every attack of the enemy on her life, and a signal to thank God for giving her to me as my wife. Note, this is when I am feeling anything but like doing that! Demonspeak will try to convince you that living against your feelings is hypocritical. This is a favourite ploy of the enemy; I have heard it many times. Verbalising and praying in line with the stated will of God is anything but hypocritical! Remember, those feelings of ours are changeable, unreliable indicators of reality. Whenever demonspeak tries to enter your mind, let God's truth pour out of your mouth. Do that consistently and see what results!

If there are things you would like to be different in your relationship, spend a period of time thanking God for your partner, calling down the blessing of God on them and rebuking every attack of the enemy on their lives. Then do a bit of a reality check on your expectations, pluck up the courage to break through that wall of silence, and begin to creatively and lovingly communicate about what you want or feel you need.

demonSPEAK

Be careful to just bring up one thing at a time, not a whole list all at once. Be very specific. If this is not the way your relationship normally operates, then don't be put off by an initially less than favourable response. You are in this for the long haul. If the issue is serious enough, you should consider getting some counselling.

> ***Reflection:*** In what ways has demonspeak begun to poison your relationship?
> What do you need to deal with in your life that is a seed of destruction in your relationship?
> What do you need to begin doing differently in your life and relationship?
> What do you need to begin talking about with your husband or wife?

UNFORGIVENESS

To forgive is to set a prisoner free and discover that the prisoner was you.

Lewis B. Smedes

I embark on this chapter conscious of the terrible, painful, inexcusable things people suffer at the hands of others, often others who should have provided safety and nurture. I write this conscious of the many tears I have cried over situations I have walked with others through.

Don't let the enemy bring harshness of judgement to you through what you read. The Holy Spirit is called the Comforter, the Helper. My prayer is that as you work through this chapter you will experience Him leading you into pathways of freedom and release from the past.

Our first chapter was entitled "It's a War Out There". It is unusual for any of us to get though life without experiencing deep hurt and disappointment at the hands of others, and also without causing deep hurt and disappointment to others and sometimes ourselves.

What are we to do with this hurt and disappointment?

I once had a picture that we are in a war and the enemy has invented a secret weapon, a gun that fires a special bullet. It hurts like anything when it first hits us. Then it lodges deep within us, releasing and even increasing the pain of the initial wound time and time again.

Unforgiveness

As already stated in this book, our real enemy is not people. Even the people who have hurt us so badly. Our real enemy is the devil and his demons. Their plan is for these hurtful events in our lives to lodge within us, taking on a life of their own, continually releasing hurt and pain. He wants to skew our picture of life and who we are through inaccurate interpretations of what happened. Going back to that earlier picture, forgiveness is about removing the bullet and preventing it from lodging itself deep within us.

Forgiveness is a central theme of the Bible. The Lord's prayer in various translations tells us to pray that God would forgive us our trespasses, sins, debts, wrongdoings, as we forgive those same things in others.

Look at this brief selection of verses:

> *Forgive us the wrongs we have done as we ourselves release forgiveness to those who have wronged us.*
> Matthew 6:12 (The Passion Translation)

> *Do not judge, and you will not be judged. Do not condemn, and you will not be condemned. Forgive, and you will be forgiven.*
>
> Luke 6:37

> *Bear with each other and forgive whatever grievances you may have against one another. Forgive as the Lord forgave you.*
>
> Colossians 3:13

> *Then Peter came to Jesus and asked, "Lord, how many times shall I forgive my brother when he sins against me? Up to seven times?" Jesus answered, "I tell you, not seven times, but seventy-seven times."*
>
> Matthew 18:21-22

In Matthew 18 some translations say seventy times seven. Now I am sure that Jesus was not giving Peter and the disciples a number to count down to before they could stop forgiving and take revenge! His clear message here is that we keep on forgiving. We make forgiveness a lifestyle.

Jesus goes on from this to tell this parable:

> *Therefore, the kingdom of heaven is like a king who wanted to settle accounts with his servants. As he began the settlement, a man who owed him ten thousand talents was brought to him. Since he was not able to pay, the master ordered that he and his wife and his children and all that he had be sold to repay the debt.*
>
> *The servant fell on his knees before him. "Be patient with me," he begged, "and I will pay back everything." The servant's master took pity on him, cancelled the debt and let him go.*
>
> *But when that servant went out, he found one of his fellow servants who owed him a hundred denarii. He grabbed him and began to choke him. "Pay back what you owe me!" he demanded.*
>
> *His fellow servant fell to his knees and begged him, "Be patient with me, and I will pay you back."*

But he refused. Instead, he went off and had the man thrown into prison until he could pay the debt. When the other servants saw what had happened, they were greatly distressed and went and told their master everything that had happened.

Then the master called the servant in. "You wicked servant," he said, "I cancelled all that debt of yours because you begged me to. Shouldn't you have had mercy on your fellow servant just as I had on you?" In anger his master turned him over to the jailers to be tortured, until he should pay back all he owed.

This is how my heavenly Father will treat each of you unless you forgive your brother from your heart.
Matthew 18:23-35

Remembering that a parable is a culturally relevant story that is told to get across a point, we are being told here that as forgiven people we are to be forgivers. Unforgiveness hinders us enjoying God's forgiveness of us, and it brings torment.

Jesus and the New Testament writers are very strong on the necessity of forgiveness. Jesus' commands and teachings are for our good. Look at these scriptures:

> *And now, O Israel, what does the Lord your God ask of you but to fear the Lord your God, to walk in all His ways, to love Him, to serve the Lord your God with all your heart and with all your soul, and to observe the Lord's commands and decrees that I am giving you today for your own good?*
> Deuteronomy 10:12-13

> *The thief comes only to steal and kill and destroy; I have come that they may have life and have it to the full.*
> John 10:10

Jesus has come to give us life in all its fullness. The enemy comes to rob kill and destroy. Jesus commands us to forgive. The enemy does all he can to make us hold on to past wrongs.

Unforgiveness is a poison that grows and festers within us.

In my work as a counsellor and a pastor I have had the privilege of working with people to help them forgive and walk into freedom from that which has held them captive for way too long. I have seen firsthand some of the tricks and lies the enemy uses to keep people in unforgiveness. Let's look at some of them together.

The enemy seeks to confuse us with a wrong understanding of what forgiveness is. Let's try to clear up some of those unhelpful thoughts.

Forgiveness is Not Reconciliation

Often, particularly in Christian circles, forgiveness is confused with reconciliation. We are confused into thinking that to forgive means to embrace the one who has hurt us so terribly, to let that person back into the inner circle of our life and expose ourselves to further harm. This understandably proves a real hindrance to forgiveness. Some people are so broken that they will almost certainly continue to cause hurt. Some are so broken that their brokenness has turned to evil. Some people need to be kept at a distance until they prove themselves safe. We can choose to forgive and leave the event behind regardless of the offender's actions, whereas reconciliation is entirely dependent on their actions.

Forgiveness is Not Minimising the Hurt

Some think that forgiveness is minimising what happened, saying that it wasn't really that bad and doesn't really matter. The truth is that real forgiveness is facing the true harm that was caused and in the light of that choosing to let it go... to forgive.

Forgiveness: Letting Them Off the Hook?

Another confusion is that forgiveness is letting the offender "off the hook". There is the thought that holding on to the hurt and offence somehow or other gets back at the one who caused it. The real truth is that the only one our unforgiveness holds "on the hook" is ourselves. Often the one who caused the pain has long forgotten it, or in some cases is now dead.

I often ask people to imagine what life will be like in ten years with this unforgiveness still alive in their lives. Will they be a better person, friend, spouse, parent, follower of Jesus? Will holding on to it increase or decrease the pain they feel? Then I ask them to imagine life in ten years without this unforgiveness present in their life.

It's Not Fair!

Most of us have struggled with this one. We feel a real need for those who have harmed us to be punished. We find ourselves crying out for personal justice, for personal vindication. This is a very natural human desire. Let not the enemy use it to keep us trapped in our pain. We live in a manifestly unjust world. It is not fair that we in my native New Zealand have so many advantages compared to many others on the planet by virtue of being born here. I wonder, too, who there is in my world that is wanting justice over something I have done!

Real forgiveness is fully acknowledging the depth of pain you have suffered, that what the offender did was totally unacceptable. It is, in that knowledge, choosing to no longer hold it against them, to let it go, to put it in a garbage container and leave it behind on the pathway of your life. In the end, forgiveness is like taking a deep breath in and then exhaling deeply, letting it all go, giving it up to Jesus, leaving that person to Jesus to sort out. Look at this scripture:

> *Do not take revenge, my friends, but leave room for God's wrath, for it is written: "It is mine to avenge; I will repay," says the Lord.*
> Romans 12:19

When I am speaking about this, I will often use the example of myself standing between a bright light and the person who has offended me. As I stand there in unforgiveness, I am shielding them from the light. As I step out of the way, the light is able to shine brightly into the situation. The scripture is telling us to get out of the way and make room for the wrath of God in the situation. Now don't get too excited with thoughts of that person being burned to a crisp by the fire of God. Even the wrath of God is redemptive by nature! But we get out of the way and allow and invite His powerful presence to be released into the situation.

The enemy will use whatever he can to keep us imprisoned, to prolong our pain and torment. Jesus comes to set us free. Jesus knows about pain and injustice. Look at Isaiah's description of Him:

> *He was despised and rejected by men,*
> *a man of sorrows, and familiar with suffering.*
> *Like one from whom men hide their faces*
> *He was despised, and we esteemed Him not.*
> Isaiah 53:3

Jesus lived His life doing good and bringing liberation to others. He poured His life into twelve men, one of whom betrayed Him. He was convicted by a cowardly judge who had found Him innocent. The crowds among whom He had done so much good had become a mob calling for His crucifixion. He was stripped, beaten and nailed to a cross. Knowing He had the power to call armies of angels to obliterate His tormentors, He instead cried out, "Father forgive them. They don't know what they are doing!" Jesus knows our pain.

One of the powerful truths about the cross is that Jesus was punished for your sin and for mine. He carried that sin. We are told He became that sin so that we could become the righteousness of God. Look at these beautiful scriptures:

> *Surely He took up our infirmities*
> *and carried our sorrows,*
> *yet we considered Him stricken by God,*
> *smitten by Him, and afflicted.*
> *But He was pierced for our transgressions,*
> *He was crushed for our iniquities;*
> *the punishment that brought us peace was*
> *upon Him,*
> *and by His wounds we are healed.*
> *We all, like sheep, have gone astray,*
> *each of us has turned to his own way;*
> *and the Lord has laid on Him the iniquity*
> *of us all.*
> Isaiah 53:4-6

> *God made Him who had no sin to be sin for us, so that in Him we might become the righteousness of God.*
> 2 Corinthians 5:21

The Cross

I remember years ago speaking with someone over an issue of forgiving herself. I encouraged her to imagine that we had been taken back to the very time when Jesus was dying on the cross. Time has been slowed right down so that she hears Him groan as each person's sin comes on Him. She is standing at the cross at the time when her sin hits Jesus and she hears Him groan. I asked her how she was going to respond as she looks up at Him. What is she going to do with this issue she can't forgive herself for? Is she going to fall on her knees in grateful worship, or is she going to say, "Thanks, but no thanks. I will continue to hold on to this"? It was a powerful moment.

I encourage you to imagine yourself there just as your sin falls on Jesus. You fall to your knees in grateful worship. Then the next person's sin that falls on Jesus is that of the person who has so deeply hurt you. What will you do with that? At the cross we are all grateful recipients of His forgiveness.

Forgive and Forget?

The enemy loves to hold us captive with the thought that we will never be able to forget what happened and therefore are unable to forgive. The scripture does not command us to forget, only to forgive. The memories will in time become manageable ones which do not immobilise and traumatise us when they come to mind. I often liken these memories and associated pain to a physical wound. Healing is a process. As we keep the wound clean, healing can occur naturally. In the same way, when we are revisited by memories and associated painful feelings, praying prayers that leave that hurtful situation with all of its pain at the cross with Jesus keeps the wound clean so that healing can continue. Pray something like this:

> *Lord Jesus I thank you that you died for me. At the cross you carried all my hurt and shame. Thank you that I have left this at the cross with you. I receive your cleansing and healing from all this pain. I give it afresh to you. I forgive this person and commit them to your redeeming power. In your mighty name Jesus. Amen.*

As we continue to walk in this healing, freedom will grow and increase in our lives.

At the end of a modern version of the movie Ben Hur, a moving story of forgiveness and reconciliation, is a song by Andra Day called "The Only Way Out" The words of the refrain are a fitting way to finish this chapter.

> *I can't hear love cause we're at war*
> *And revenge is so loud and the drums are so proud*
> *But oh, I'm in a cage and I hear mercy say*
> *"I'm here now"*
> *And it's the only way out*
> *I can't hear love cause we're at war*
> *But revenge is so loud and the drums are so proud*
> *But I'm still in a cage and I hear mercy say now*
> *It's the only way*
> *Mercy's the only way out*
> *Mercy gave me my way out*

Reflection: In what ways has demonspeak held you captive to past hurt?
What specific steps will you take to step into forgiveness and freedom?

Note: All of the above does not necessarily mean not taking legal action in regard to past injustices. Some people need to be confronted and even taken out of circulation for the safety of others.

CONCLUSION

Remembering my sister's encouragement, and with some vague feelings of incompleteness, I now finish this book. I could continue writing and go on to examine the place of demonspeak as it relates to fear of failure (or success), self-esteem, anger, and a myriad of other facets of life. Of course, that list of further possible chapters could prove to be the very demonspeak that prevents me from ever completing this book!

My hope and earnest prayer is that you will have become much more aware of your thoughts and their origins, that you will be diligent in taking them captive, and that you will try doing some journaling, capturing them on paper and counteracting them with His truth from your *Liberation Manual*. My heart is excited by the idea of you declaring war on thoughts that have held you captive for years, and the freedom you will find as you overcome them.

I would love to hear any questions, comments and reflections you may have. Feel free to email me at liberationmanual@gmail.com. My original vision was that this would be the first in a series of writings called *Freedom Insights*. I will need to get faster at turning them out as I am now 68 years old.

demonSPEAK

I bless you in Jesus' name with a free mind and a liberated heart that will in turn bless others around you!

Again, yahoo!

Have fun.

Enjoy your journey into freedom.

In Jesus' Name!

G

www.ingramcontent.com/pod-product-compliance
Lightning Source LLC
Chambersburg PA
CBHW070303010526
44108CB00039B/1647